South Africa's
Winelands

A VISITOR'S GUIDE

TANITH HOBSON & JOHN COLLINS

Struik Publishers (Pty) Ltd
(a member of The Struik Publishing Group (Pty) Ltd)
Cornelis Struik House, 80 McKenzie Street, Cape Town 8001

Reg. No.: 54/00965/07

First published in 1997

2 4 6 8 10 9 7 5 3

ISBN 1 86872 100 0

Managing editor: Annlerie van Rooyen
Editor: Claudia Dos Santos
Editorial assistant: Cara Neville
Designer: Laurence Lemmon-Warde
Cartographer: John Collins
Cartographic editor: Desiree Oosterberg
Project co-ordinator: Glynne Newlands
Proofreader and indexer: Simon Pooley

Reproduction: Hirt & Carter Cape (Pty) Ltd
Printing and binding by NBD,
Drukkery Street, Goodwood 7460, Western Cape

ACKNOWLEDGEMENTS
This publication would not have been possible without the generous assistance, advice and encouragement given by so
many people, and we would especially like to thank all the wine farms and estates that made this book possible.
We would also like to express our sincere appreciation to all the wine route trusts and tourism bureaux whose
co-operation and communication with the wine farms and estates has proved invaluable.
We would especially like to thank Posy and Jeremy Hazel for their hard work and enthusiasm, and Peta Vella for all her help
and input. Also the KWV Head Office and Media Centre who have generously given of their time, knowledge and expertise.
Our gratitude to Struik Publishers who put this book together, especially to Annlerie, who believed in our idea,
and Claudia, for all her patience and hard work.
And lastly, to our very dear friends and family, we would like to express our warmest
gratitude for their constant encouragement and support.

Although every effort has been made to ensure factual accuracy in this book, the Publishers will not be held responsible for any
changes that may occur at the time of going to press. The author and Publishers invite any comments or suggestions for future
updates by writing to: The Editor, *South Africa's Winelands*, Struik Publishers (Pty) Ltd, P O Box 1144, Cape Town 8000.

Publishers' note: • Not all of the wines mentioned in this book may be available to the public.
• Due to space constraints this publication is not a comprehensive listing of all the
wine farms/estates/co-operatives in South Africa.

Front cover: Groot Constantia (Mark Skinner); *Back cover:* Hex River Valley (Colour Library/SIL);
Spine: Lanzerac Manor House (Mark Skinner/SIL); *Front flap:* Thelema Cellars (courtesy Thelema Estate);
Back flap: Zevenwacht homestead (courtesy Zevenwacht Estate).

CONTENTS

Although historical records indicate that wine was first made some 7 000 years ago, few facts are known about the origins of this industry. It is, however, generally accepted that the first wine was made in Asia Minor, especially in the Caucasus area and Mesopotamia.

From there, wine making spread to Egypt, where hieroglyphic evidence has been found dating back to around 5 000 BC. By 2 000 BC the ancient Greeks and Cretans, too, were making wine. Around 1 000 BC, vineyards had been planted in what is today Sicily and Italy, as well as in the north African countries. As little as 500 years later, the art of wine making had spread as far as Spain, Arabia and the south of France. Northern China and India began to make wine around 100 BC and, shortly after that, the wine making industry had taken hold in the Balkan states and in Northern Europe.

For the next 1 000 years, the expansion of the wine industry ground to a virtual halt, due largely to the decline of the Roman Empire. It was only during the 16th century, that it was carried farther afield. By 1530 vineyards had been planted in Mexico as well as Japan. In 1560 Argentina imported vines, followed by Peru.

The next milestone was the planting of the first vineyards at the Cape of Good Hope in 1655. California followed in 1697 and New Zealand as late as 1813.

In 1652, the Dutch East India Company established a refreshment station at the Cape of Good Hope, with the aim of providing fresh produce for the company's merchant vessels on their long voyages to and from the Indies.

The climate at the tip of Africa was ideal and the ground fertile, and only a few years later wine making emerged as a flourishing secondary industry – and sailors began referring to Cape Town as the 'Tavern of the Seas'.

Jan van Riebeeck, the first governor, had planted a vineyard at the Cape in 1655, and on 2 February 1659 the first wine was pressed.

Expansion followed and soon vines were planted on a larger scale at Bosch-heuvel (today the suburbs of Wynberg and Bishopscourt). Although encouraged by van Riebeeck, the early Dutch farmers were reluctant to plant vines, due to their lack of knowledge of viticulture.

Things improved when Simon van der Stel succeeded van Riebeeck in 1679. This new governor, a wine enthusiast who knew about vines and the art of wine making, was soon producing some good wine on his farm in the Constantia Valley.

But the local wine industry really only began to flourish when a group of religious refugees from France settled at the Cape between 1680 and 1690. The French Huguenots arrived almost penniless, but they brought with them their rich wine making heritage and a wealth of skills, which they learnt to adapt to the new conditions at the Cape.

The zeal and expertise of the Huguenots boosted South Africa's fledgling wine making industry, leaving an impression that is still tangible today, especially in towns like Franschhoek.

The 18th century presented a difficult phase for Cape wine makers. Resistance on the export market was mainly due to the poor quality of the product, which, in turn, was caused by factors such as a critical shortage of oak vats, needed to age the wines properly. Furthermore, the Cape wine growers were struggling to adapt proven wine making techniques to local conditions and to identify the cultivars best suited for each district. This was not an easy task, as the Cape province provides tremendous variety, both in terrain and climatic conditions. Desert along the West Coast gives way to vast stretches of semi-arid land in the centre, open grassland in the east, and folded mountains in the south.

The first half of the 19th century brought an unexpected windfall – Britain's occupation of the Cape, and the war between Britain and France, created a large new market for Cape wines.

Within the following 45 years, the Cape's production increased from 0,5 million to 4,5 million litres of wine per annum. However, little attention was paid to quality and planning, and when Britain and France made peace in 1881, the South African market collapsed.

Due to massive overproduction, low prices and the outbreak of phylloxera disease, many wine farmers faced bankruptcy, while others turned to more lucrative ventures like ostrich farming.

Only in 1918, with the establishment of the Ko-operatiewe Wijnbouwers Vereeniging van Zuid Afrika Beperkt (the KWV), were order and security restored and the foundations for today's wine industry laid.

The KWV, established by the farmers themselves, has proved itself a capable governing body and champion of the wine growers' interests. This dynamic commercial organisation markets the wines of the country internationally, acts as administrator of the wine industry at producer level, and offers a wide range of specialist services – both to support the wine farmers and to introduce the public to the arts of vini- and viticulture. It is also the largest exporter of wine and brandy in South Africa.

The Cape wine growing areas are situated in a relatively narrow zone, but produce some of the world's most outstanding wines.

The area has a Mediterranean climate perfect for the cultivation of vines. Cool, misty winters with plentiful rainfall are followed by long, sunny summer days needed for the ripening of the grapes. The mountain slopes and valleys form the ideal habitat for the wine grape, vitis vinifera, whose products have given pleasure to man for many centuries.

WHITE WINES

Bukettraube
Developed in Germany; produces quality wines with a muscat aroma.

Cape Riesling
A shy bearer which produces one of South Africa's best quality white wines, if growth and ripening conditions are ideal. A delicate, yet fruity, bouquet and sharp grassy aroma. The variety, for many years wrongly regarded as Weisser (Rhine) Riesling, was later identified as the Crouchen blanc of France.

Chardonnay
Noble variety from which the famous white wines of Burgundy are made; also used in the production of Chablis wines and Champagne. Locally, high quality wines are made and often aged in wood to bring out the best characteristics. The high fruit sugar content of this variety lends itself to good ageing potential. It is increasingly used by Cape winemakers as the basis of Cap Classique sparkling wines.

Chenel
A local crossing between Chenin blanc and Ugni blanc which produces a white wine of reasonable quality.

Chenin Blanc (Steen)
The most widely planted grape variety in the Cape. A very versatile variety that produces good natural wines covering the entire spectrum from sweet to dry, sherry, as well as sparkling wine; also used for distilling brandy and spirits.

Clairette Blanche
A favourite among South African winemakers, very low in alcohol and acid content. Although seldom used as single variety, its presence is essential in many of the light, fruity wines produced locally.

Colombar(d)
Planted especially in the Breede River region, this cultivar produces a quality wine in the warmer areas. Good acid content ensures fresh, interesting wines with a pleasant fruity flavour.

Emerald Riesling
A relatively new variety from California which made its commercial debut in 1981. The wine is flavourful and fruity.

Gewürztraminer
A prominent spicy flavour and taste, usually produces a light, off-dry wine.

Muscat d'Alexandrie (Hanepoot)
One of the world's most widely planted grapes, in South Africa, it is used mainly for dessert wine, as well as natural wine and raisins, it forms a high percentage of the total grape harvest. Hanepoot gives a strong, flowery bouquet, and an intense honey flavour.

DICTIONARY OF GRAPES AND WINES

Muscadel

A member of the muscat family, used chiefly in dessert wines, to which it imparts an intense, raisin-like bouquet. Red and white grapes are grown mainly in the Breede River region.

Palomino (White French grape)

A heavy bearer, low in sugar content and acid. This variety is used mainly for the making of sherry and brandy. It produces a neutral wine that is best enjoyed young.

Pinot Gris

Planted on a very small scale in South Africa. The wines it produces are full and well-balanced.

Sauvignon Blanc

In combination with semillon and muscadel these grapes produce some of the most exceptional white wines of the Bordeaux region (France), including the sweetest Sauternes and driest Graves. This variety is generally recognisable by its peppery, grassy character. It is often aged in wood.

Semillon (Green Grape)

It produces a full yet subtle wine with little acid and is often used in blends.

Ugni Blanc (Trebbiano)

Neutral wines which are used almost exclusively in the production of brandy.

Weisser Riesling (Rhine Riesling)

This is one of the world's most noble varieties. In South Africa it produces superb, full, flavourful wines with excellent fruit acids, that develop well with bottle ageing.

RED WINES

Cabernet Franc

This cultivar is related to Cabernet Sauvignon, from which it is not easily distinguished. It is usually softer, has a lower sugar content and contains less alcohol. Unless specified, Cabernet refers to Sauvignon, not to Franc.

Cabernet Sauvignon

Produces top-class wines and is the foremost variety produced by the Bordeaux region of France. With age, it develops into a spicy, full and complex wine. It is often blended with soft red wines for early drinking.

Cinsaut

A strong bearer and very versatile variety, known previously as Hermitage. It can be blended with the most noble of Cabernets, or produce the most modest and low-priced wine, light and ready for early drinking. It is also a quality wine for brandy distilling, and frequently used for rosé, port and Jerepigo wines. At present, this is the most widely planted red variety, but is fast being replaced by more noble cultivars.

Gamay Noir

In France, light red wines in the Beaujolais style are made of the Gamay grape. Some reds are made locally in the nouveau, or young wine, style.

Merlot

This variety is used especially to soften blended wines. Its ability to age faster than Cabernet makes it useful for softening Cabernet wines.

Muscadel

Red Muscadel forms an important part of the famous Constantia dessert wines. In the Klein Karoo this light red variety produces a very popular, sweet red wine.

Pinotage

This local crossing between Pinot Noir and Cinsaut (Hermitage) often has an acetone character, is full and fruity and needs as little as two to three years to reach its peak.

Pinot Noir

The most important variety of the French Burgundy and Champagne regions, it produces local wines with excellent berry character and bouquet, as well as a rounded taste. Pinot Noir grapes are also used in sparkling wine.

Shiraz

This, too, is a variety of French origin. The largest production of Shiraz is now found in Australia. It is a noble variety, which gives a deep purple wine that develops a complex and outspoken character with age.

Souzão

Originally from Portugal, the high fruit sugar content and strongly pigmented skin of this cultivar guarantees excellent colour and taste. It is regarded as one of the better port varieties.

Tinta Barocca

One of the very best varieties for the production of port in South Africa, it also produces earthy, organic red wines and is excellent for blending.

Zinfandel

This variety is planted on a limited scale in South Africa. Its product is of average colour and body, with a characteristic bouquet and fruity aroma.

RIGHT The quality wines of Backsberg Estate in the Paarl Valley mature in these large wooden caskets.
(Peter Pickford/Struik Image Library)

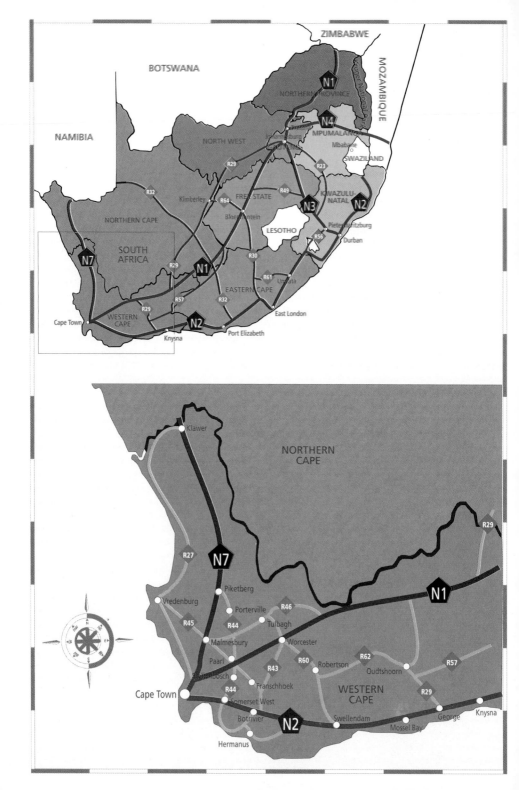

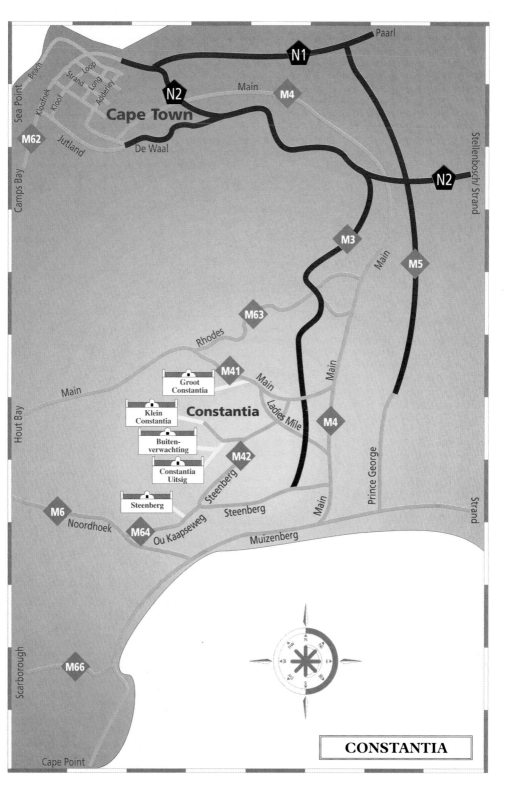

CONSTANTIA

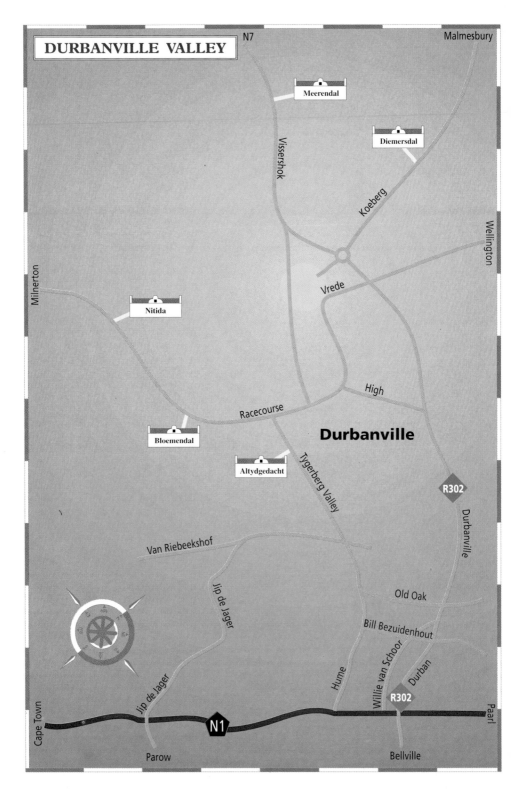

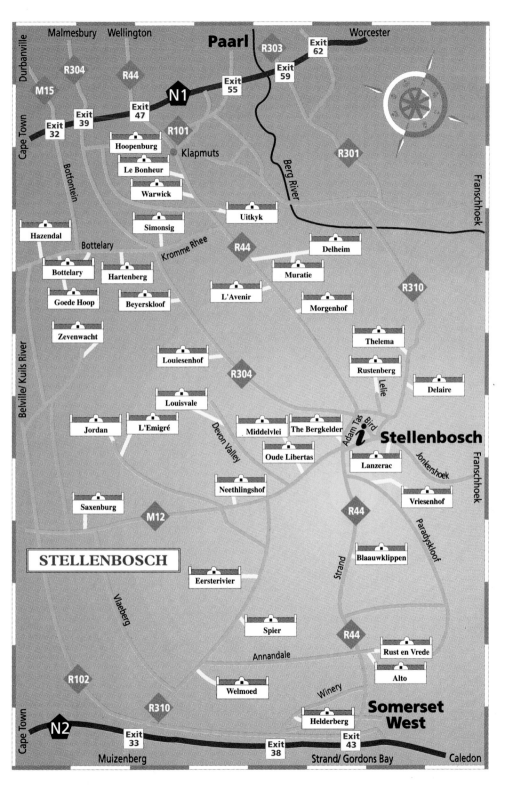

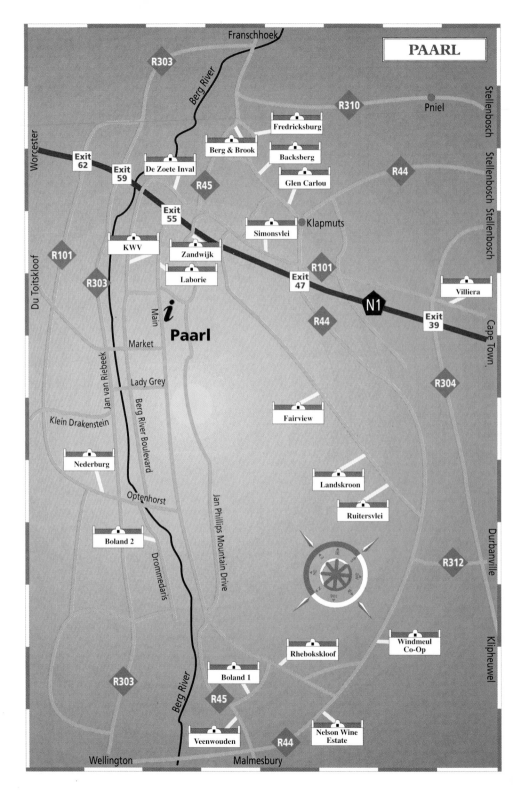

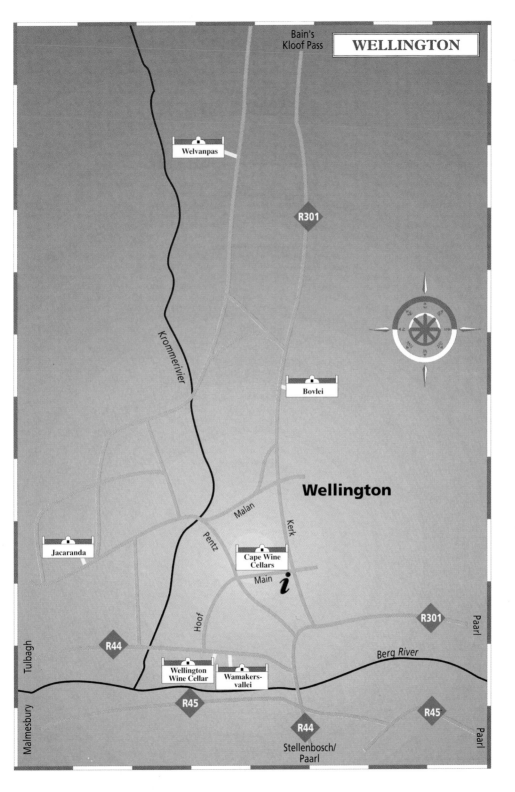

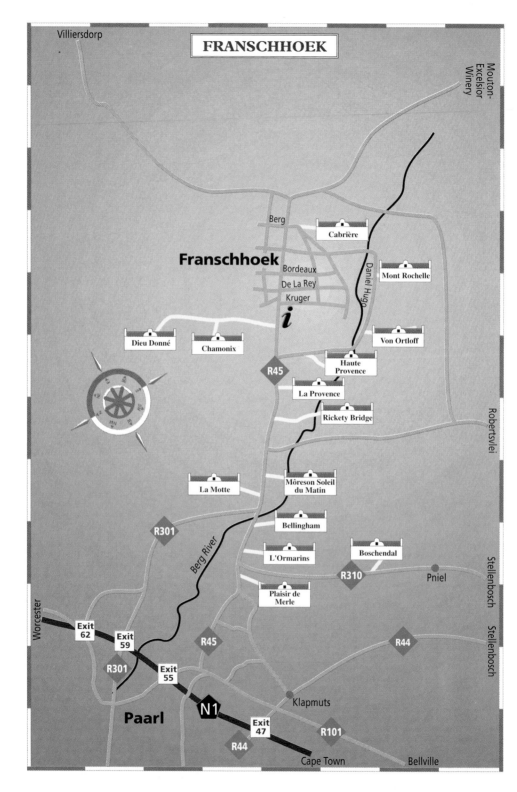

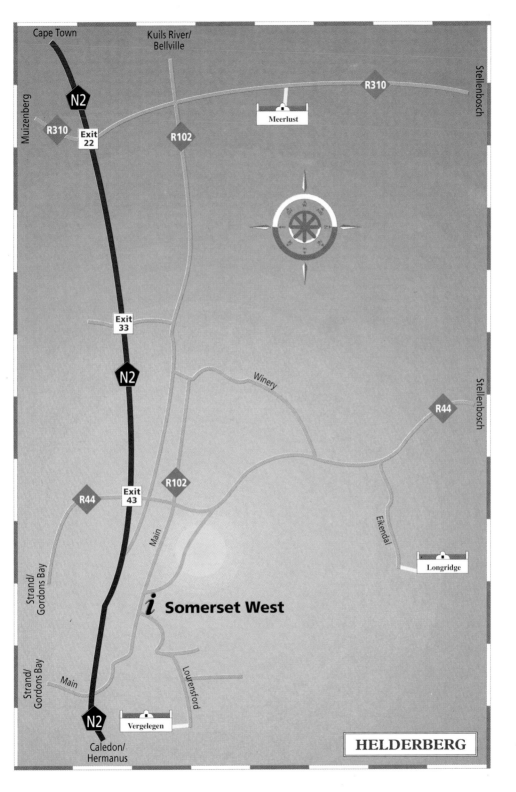

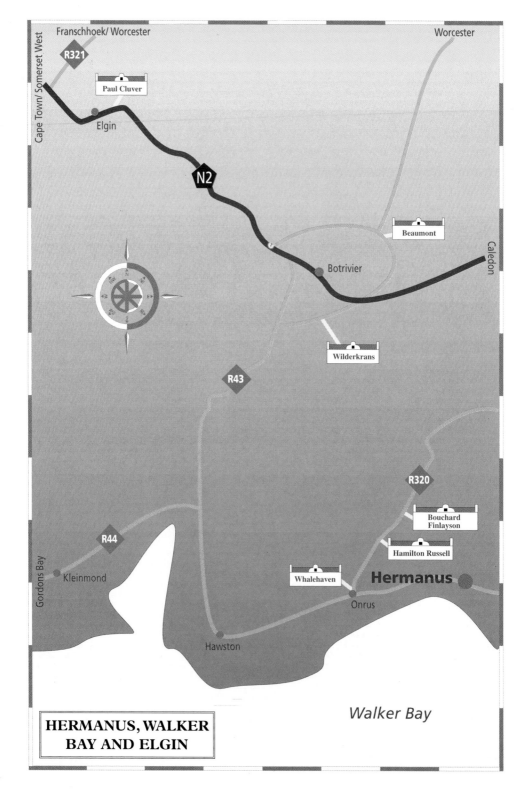

HERMANUS, WALKER
BAY AND ELGIN

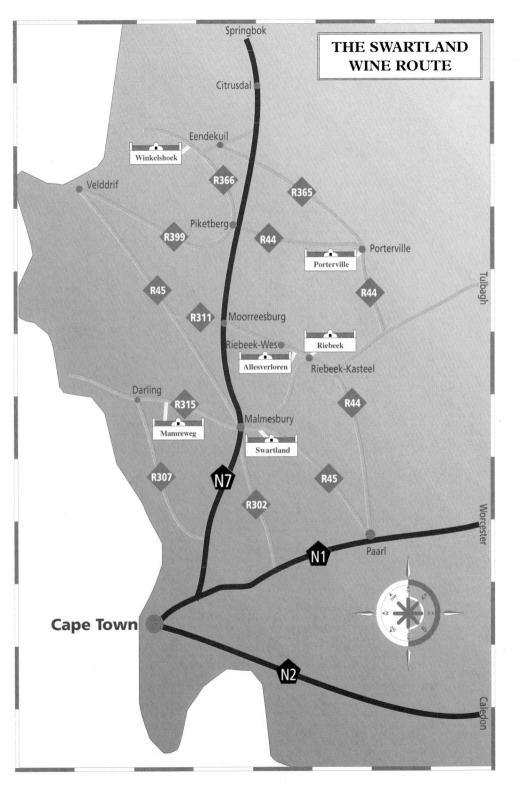

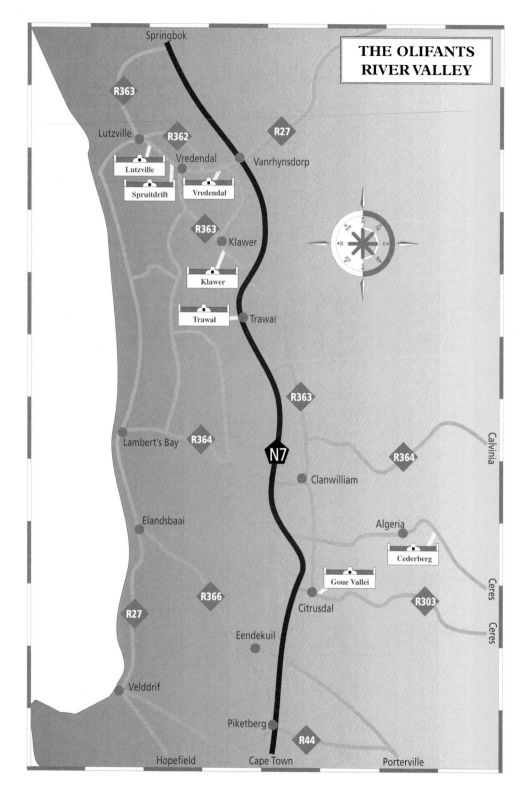

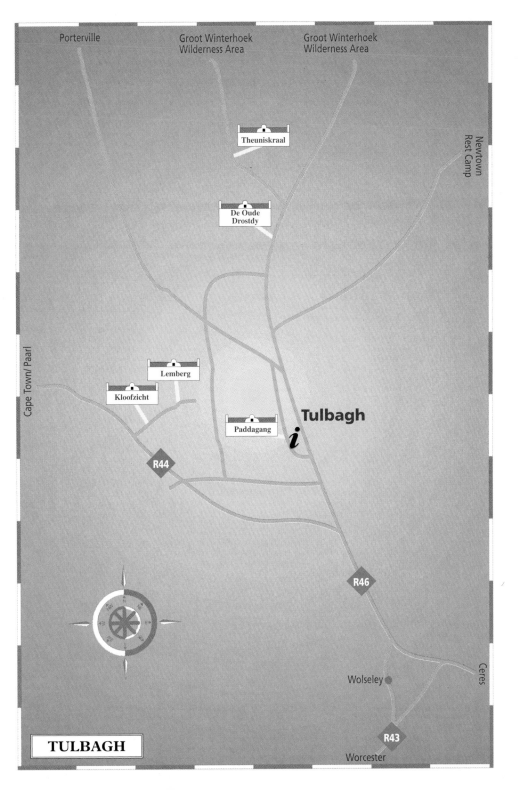

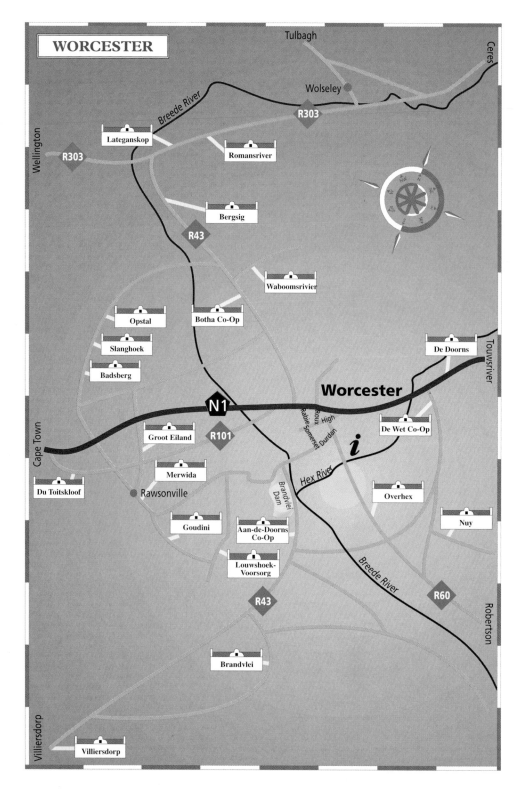

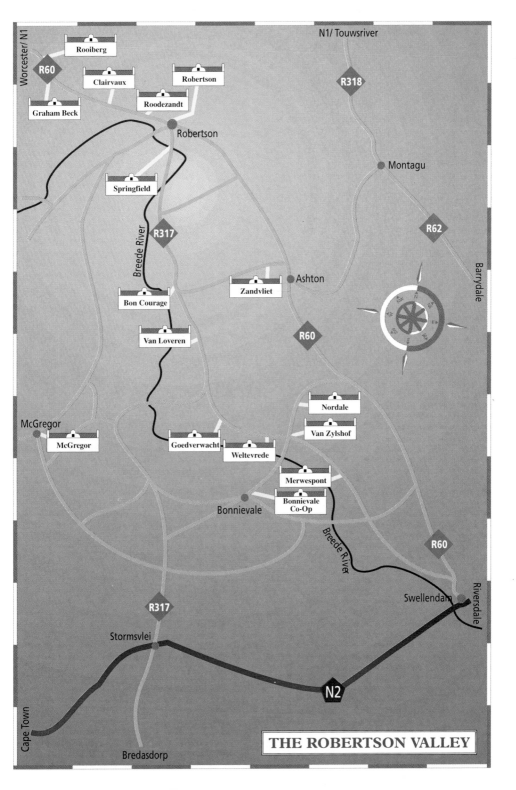

THE ROBERTSON VALLEY

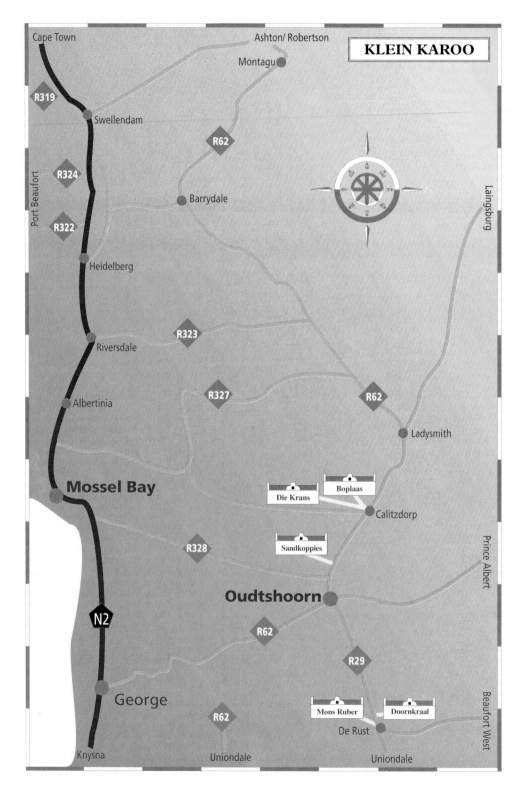

Wine, as are most things in life, is enjoyed by the senses, the combination of aroma, colour and taste creating a unique experience of pleasure.

The colour of a wine can tell you a great deal about its variety, age and quality. Wine should be attractive and lively and must be absolutely clear.

Every wine has a unique smell, also called nose. Wine should radiate the specific fragrance of the variety of grape from which it was made.

Two important characteristics can be detected by tasting the wine. The first is the 'fullness' (weight), which has to do with the intensity of the sensation in the mouth. The second is the 'farewell', or the time its taste lingers in the mouth after swallowing. The longer the pleasant taste lingers, the better the wine.

Wine is the only natural drink that was created to be enjoyed with food. This applies to table wine, as well as fortified wines which are made for drinking before a meal (sherry and vermouth), during a meal (natural table wine), or after a meal (port, dessert wine and brandy).

Although no one should be restrained by rules about which wine should be drunk with which food, centuries of experience in these matters have resulted in tried and tested guidelines. For those who don't, as yet, have their own opinions about which wine goes with which food, these guidelines can pave the way to an enjoyable experience.

According to an age-old code, vermouth and sherry (dry and off-dry) are drunk as an aperitif before a meal. Sweet sherry is best enjoyed with dessert.

White wine usually accompanies the more delicate dishes such as fish, while the heavier red wines go well with meals like beef, venison and composite dishes.

Dry wines are drunk before sweet ones, and white before red when there is more than one wine served with the meal. Rosé, a multipurpose wine, is served between the white and red wine. Sweet wine is drunk after a meal, with dessert or fruit. In South Africa, port is usually served at the end of a meal, and sometimes liqueur or liqueur brandy.

Sparkling wine, traditionally served on festive occasions, can be enjoyed at any stage of the meal.

There are also well-tried recommendations about the temperatures at which wine should be served.

Rosé and whites are cooled, though never served ice cold as sudden temperature fluctuations can be detrimental to the taste of wine. Red wine is served at room temperature. (But, since this rule applies to the European climate of 20–30°C, it may be necessary to cool red wines slightly in hot South Africa). Sparkling wine is cooled in the ice bucket from which it is served, and vermouth is usually served with crushed ice. Port and white dessert wine are served at room temperature. Sherry and dessert wine can be cooled in summer.

The picturesque Constantia Valley is not only South Africa's oldest wine growing area, it is regarded by many to be the country's premier wine region.

Here, on the slopes of the mountains which form the backbone of the Cape Peninsula, from Table Mountain to Cape Point, nature has provided almost ideal growing conditions for wine grapes – long days of sunlight, a temperate climate with plentiful winter rain, cool ocean breezes and a variety of soil types.

Perhaps it was the gentle climate that prompted the early European settlers to plant vines between the granite ridges and the sea, but, whatever the reason, it became evident that this was an inspired decision. The vines flourished and the wines of the Constantia Valley soon became a much sought-after commodity.

Groot Constantia, the best known of the Cape Dutch homesteads, stands on the site of former Dutch governor Simon van der Stel's country home. The farm, then much larger, was presented to him in 1685 by a visiting commissioner, HA van Rheede tot Drakenstein, as reward for his outstanding work and service. Since the Commissioner's young daughter was called Constantia, the farm was probably named after her.

Four years after van der Stel's death in 1712, the farm was divided into smaller sections, and the area containing the homestead became known as Groot Constantia. For three generations it prospered under the ownership of the Cloete family. In 1860 it was sold to the Cape government as an experimental wine farm. Although a fire destroyed the homestead in 1925, it was duly restored on the instructions of the South African government.

Every Saturday and Sunday throughout the year an Antiques and Collectables Fair is held at Groot Constantia.

For visitors wishing to browse for edibles, there are shopping areas such as the Constantia Uitsig Farmstall, Old Cape Farmstall, Barnyard Egg and Constantia Village, which offer all the necessary goods as well as freshly baked bread, fresh fruit and vegetables, homemade preserves, farm honey and more.

Also nestled in this charming valley are a number of exquisite accommodation establishments, some of which are rated among the best in the world. One such place is the Cellars-Hohenhort Hotel, situated on 3.6 ha (9 acres) of lovely, landscaped gardens with sweeping views of the Constantia Valley and False Bay. The splendid manor house and the magnificently restored wine cellar feature 53 rooms, including a variety of suites. The two elegant restaurants are noted for their fine cuisine.

Many other fine restaurants are situated in this valley, attracting locals and tourists alike. Elegant Constantia with its broad, oak-lined avenues, is well worth a visit.

BUITENVERWACHTING

Buitenverwachting originally formed part of the Constantia Estate, founded by Simon van der Stel. This beautiful piece of land changed hands often, yet flourished as a wine farm thanks to the 90 000 vines planted in 1825 by Ryk Arnoldus Cloete, brother of the famous Hendrik Cloete of Constantia. From 1866 the fortunes of Buitenverwachting were inextricably linked with those of the Louw and Lategan families, after Danie Lategan's daughter Olivia, born at Buitenverwachting, married George Louw.

The farm was lovingly restored to its former glory, while extensive planting of the most selected of cultivars was initiated. The result was a maiden grape harvest of 98 tons in 1985 for the 'new' Buitenverwachting, the first harvest in 30 years. An historic achievement that lived up to the estate's name – Buitenverwachting, 'Beyond Expectation'.

The concept of environment-friendly farming has been introduced to the 75 ha (185-acre) vineyard and the modern cellar features some of the most up-to-date wine making equipment available.

Consistently rated among the top ten restaurants in the country, the fare at Buitenverwachting ranges from noble continental to traditional South African dishes in an exclusive venue overlooking the vineyards.

BEVERAGES INCLUDE:
Buiten Blanc, Rhine Riesling and Brût.

Opening times:
09:00 – 17:00 seven days a week.
• Cellar tours by appointment.

Buitenverwachting
Klein Constantia Road
Constantia
7800
P.O. Box 281
Constantia
7847

Tel: (021) 794 5190/1
Fax: (021) 794 1351
Restaurant Tel: (021) 794 3522

In 1881 Stephanus Petrus Lategan came to the Constantia valley and bought a considerable piece of Buitenverwachting farmland from Johannes Wynand Louw. Later, Stephanus Lategan acquired Buitenverwachting itself, as well as enough of the surrounding land to give fine farms to his four sons. Constantia Uitsig (View), which went to Willem Hendrik, was the only one of the four farms that lacked an imposing homestead and was still only open veld. No doubt Stephanus was well aware of his son's drive, for Willem soon turned his land into a model farm.

In 1894 Willem married Antoinette Bredell of Schoemanshoek, and with her inheritance built the present homestead of Constantia Uitsig. He was an industrious farmer. His first revenue seems to have been derived from fruit.

Then, approximately eight years before the turn of the century, viticulture in the Constantia Valley received a stimulus when the Union-Castle Shipping Company installed refrigeration in some of its ships. In 1896 Willem Lategan became the first South African farmer to export his table grapes to London.

In 1988 the farm was purchased by David McCay and his wife Marlene. Together they restored it to its former glory. Wine making has recently been revived on the farm and at present there are 40 ha (99 acres) under cultivation. Constantia Uitsig Hotel offers gracious seclusion to the discerning traveller. Accommodation consists of 15 luxurious garden suites. The restaurant expertly prepares widely varied Mediterranean provincial cuisine, while the wine list offers the best of the Cape. The hotel also has its own private cricket oval – one of only two in the country.

La Colombe restaurant offers exquisite French cuisine in an intimate setting.

BEVERAGES INCLUDE:
Semillon, La Colombe Vin Blanc, Sauvignon Blanc, Chardonnay and Cabernet Sauvignon Merlot.

Opening times:
Weekdays: 09:30 – 17:00
Saturdays: 09:30 – 13:30
• Wines can be purchased from the Centre at the entrance of the estate.
• Local and worldwide deliveries by arrangement.

Constantia Uitsig
P.O. Box 32
Constantia
7848

Tel: (021) 794 1810
Fax: (021) 794 1812

Constantia Uitsig Farm
Tel: (021) 794 6500
Fax: (021) 794 7605

GROOT CONSTANTIA

Groot Constantia is where the roots of South Africa's wine industry lie. This estate, the oldest in the country, was developed by Simon van der Stel who received it as a gift in 1685. Since then, Groot Constantia has an uninterrupted record as a wine farm and its name is irrevocably linked to the most famous wines ever produced in South Africa.

Today the estate is owned by the Groot Constantia Trust, a company without gain, whose main objectives are to preserve this beautiful and historic estate for posterity and to honour the name of South African wine. Groot Constantia produces a range of award-winning wines, excelling in reds as well as whites.

Of the two restaurants on the estate, the Groot Constantia Tavern Restaurant offers continental dishes, while Jonkerhuis Restaurant specialises in original Cape cuisine.

The Estate offers wine tastings and sales, a museum in the magnificent manor house, a beautiful historic cellar with a sculptured pediment gable, an art gallery and two gift shops.

BEVERAGES INCLUDE:
Chardonnay Reserve, Chardonnay, Sauvignon Blanc, Kommandeurs Blanc, Gewürztraminer, Weisser Riesling, Bouquet Blanc, Gouverneurs Reserve, Cabernet Sauvignon, Shiraz, Shiraz/Merlot, Pinotage, Constantia Rood and Port.

Opening times:
10:00 – 17:00 seven days a week.
• Closed on Christmas Day, New Year's Day and Good Friday.
• Opening hours change during high season, so please call the estate for information.
• Cellar tours every hour from 10:00 – 16:00.

Groot Constantia Estate
Private Bag
Constantia
7848

Tel: (021) 794 5128
Fax: (021) 794 1999

With its historic Cape Dutch homestead and superb views across the valley and False Bay, Klein Constantia, some 20 minutes by car from Cape Town, has frequently been described as one of the world's most beautiful vineyard locations.

The estate forms part of the land granted to Simon van der Stel in 1685. This early Dutch governor of the Cape planted the first vineyards in Constantia, which later produced the legendary Constantia dessert wine. Requested by Napoleon and praised in the writings of Charles Dickens and Jane Austen, this wine was sought after by the European élite of the 18th and 19th centuries.

Klein Constantia Estate was rather run down when bought in 1980 by Duggie Jooste, whose family has been involved in the South African wine trade for four generations. His son, Lowell, after qualifying as a chartered accountant, spent a year studying viticulture and oenology (the study of wine) at the University of California, Davis. Afterwards he worked the 1987 harvest at Robert Mondavi Winery in the Napa Valley. Today, both Duggie and Lowell are involved in the day-to-day running of Klein Constantia Estate.

Vineyard upgrading started in 1982 and today the entire estate has been replanted (70 per cent of the plantings are white grapes). 75 ha (185 acres) of the farm are under vines ranging from 90–300 m (295–984 ft) above sea level.

The low, warmer northfacing slopes are ideal for reds, while the cool, higher southfacing slopes favour the whites. Rainfall is high throughout and no irrigation is necessary. All Klein Constantia's wines are grown, made and bottled on the estate.

Klein Constantia winemaker, Ross Gower, was declared Wine Man of the Year in John Platter's 1991 SA Wine Guide.

BEVERAGES INCLUDE:
Sauvignon Blanc, Chardonnay, Rhine Riesling, Cabernet Sauvignon, Shiraz, Marlbrook (a blend of Cabernet Sauvignon, Merlot and Cabernet Franc), Shiraz and Vin de Constance.

Opening times:
Weekdays: 09:00 – 17:00
Saturdays: 09:00 – 13:00

Klein Constantia Estate
P.O. Box 375
Constantia
7848

Tel: (021) 794 5188
Fax: (021) 794 2464

Steenberg, once known as 'Zwaaneweide' or 'Zwaanswyk', was the first land grant made in the Constantia Valley in 1682. The land originally went to a young widow, Catherina Ras, and wines were first produced here in 1695.

Today, some 300 years later, the historic *werf* (original homestead) has been painstakingly restored in the style of an 18th-century farm. The farmstead, including the manor house and other buildings, has been declared a national monument in terms of the War Graves and National Monument Act of 1969. The main gable, a *holbol* (convex-concave) outlined by heavy mouldings in a small keystone, is the only surviving example of its type in the Cape Peninsula.

This prime wine estate has now been developed to include an exquisite country hotel, an 18-hole championship golf course and a residential development.

The guiding principle behind Steenberg Vineyards, which produced its first vintage of Sauvignon Blanc in 1992, is quality, not quantity. Since 1990, some 64 ha (158 acres) have been planted with carefully selected grape varieties. Much care has been taken in the selection and planting process to ensure that vines produce to their finest potential. Each variety has been ideally matched with a specific soil type, slope and micro-climate. Then, with minimal human intervention, nature is allowed to take her course. In the cellar, as in the vineyard, every process is kept as natural as possible.

BEVERAGES INCLUDE:
Sauvignon Blanc, Chardonnay, Semillon, Merlot, Pinot Noir, Cabernet Sauvignon, Cabernet Franc, Shiraz and Nebbiolo.

Opening times:
Weekdays: 09:30 – 16:00
Saturdays: 09:00 – 12:00

Steenberg Vineyards
P.O. Box 10801
Steenberg Estate
Cape Town
7945

Tel: (021) 713 2211
Fax: (021) 713 2201

Three centuries ago, the fertile soil of the Durbanville hills and surrounding areas was chosen to produce the vegetables, fruit, meat and wine that would replenish the Dutch East India Company ships calling at the Cape of Good Hope on their way to the East.

Today, the Durbanville Wine Valley, just 20 km (12 miles) out of Cape Town, is still producing superior crops. Together with Constantia, it has the distinction of being the region with the best climate for wine grape production in South Africa.

One of the coolest wine growing areas in the world (Region 2 on the International heat summation scale), it averages only around 19°C (66°F) between September and March. The ripening period of the grapes is further lengthened by late summer mists and the cooling winds off the Atlantic Ocean 16 km (10 miles) away.

Even the so-called Cape Doctor (southeasterly gales off False Bay) works in favour of the valley, tempering the humidity in which vine diseases would otherwise flourish.

A wide selection of slope aspects allows for optimum matching of cultivar to terroir. The rich red soils in the area are predominantly of the Hutton and Clovelly type; deep, cool and well drained, but with a good water-holding capacity. This, together with the heavy localised dews, means

that vineyards can be cultivated without irrigation, even though the average annual rainfall in the area is only 550 mm (22 in).

The character and stature of grapes grown in this valley have long been acknowledged by the wine making fraternity, who source these grapes to make many well known and respected wines. However, it is only fairly recently that the farms in the area have started to make an impressive name as wine-makers in their own right, with wines bottled under their own labels.

A wide variety of wines are offered, from the noble red and white cultivars to the well loved and unique Altydgedacht Barbera. All 5 cellars in the Durbanville Valley – Altydgedacht, Bloemendal, Diemersdal, Meerendal and Nitida, have recently won Veritas gold medals, a fact bearing witness to the quality of the valley's wines.

The farms are well known for the distinctive fruity wines they produce, and are open for visiting and tasting during the week.

Tygerberg Tourism
P.O. Box 100
Durbanville
7551

Tel: (021) 96 3453
Fax: (021) 975 2579

ALTYDGEDACHT

Altydgedacht, on the slopes of the fertile Tygerberg Hills, is one of the oldest wine farms in the Cape with an unbroken tradition of wine making over the last 290 years. The cellar was built in 1705 and old inventories show that the farm sold wine to wholesalers in 1730. However, the first wines to appear under the Altydgedacht Estate label were released as recently as 1985.

History is tangible on this beautiful estate. The title deeds granting the farm to Elsje van Suurwaarde in 1698, signed by Cape governor Simon van der Stel, are on view. The tasting room is hung with portraits from the past – one is of Count de Las Cases (the secretary and fellow inmate of Napoleon Bonaparte) who, in 1815, stayed on the farm en-route from St Helena to France.

The farm has been in the Parker family for five generations, thanks to the determination and courage of their women. The widowed grandmother, Daisy, ran it herself while her three sons were away in World War II. And for the last five decades, Jean Parker, widowed in 1954 when her sons were both under four years old, has run the farm, becoming one of South Africa's first female winemakers.

The Parker family has farmed Altydgedacht since the middle of the last century and has long been a valued supplier of top quality grapes, first to Monis (SFW), and then specifically for the Nederburg range. Recently, they won Veritas gold medals for the 1996 Sauvignon Blanc, 1994 Pinotage and the unique Barbera. The 1995 Pinotage was voted Wine Magazine's Champion Pinotage for that vintage.

The success of the estate is attributable not only to the exceptional climate, but also to brothers Oliver and John Parker, both qualified viticulturists and oenologists, with working experience in the Napa Valley, New Zealand and Australia.

BEVERAGES INCLUDE:
Chatelaine, Gewürztraminer, Sauvignon Blanc, Chardonnay, Shiraz, and Cabernet Sauvignon.

Opening times:
Weekdays: 09:00 – 17:30
Saturdays: 09:00 – 13:00
• Closed on Sundays and religious holidays.
• Cellar tours by appointment.
• Pampoenkraal outdoor restaurant open October – April.

Altydgedacht
P.O. Box 213
Durbanville
7551

Tel: (021) 96 1295
Fax: (021) 96 8521

Bloemendal farm is almost 300 years old. It was bought in the late 1800s by the great-grandfather of the current owner, Jackie Coetzee, to farm sheep, cattle, a little wheat and sweet potatoes. His grandfather, Jannie van der Westhuizen, built the cellar in 1920, but it was his father, Koos Coetzee who started planting significant amounts of Cabernet Sauvignon and Shiraz in the early 1960s.

As part of Die Kloof, up the road from Altydgedacht, Bloemendal today boasts vineyards with varying aspects – provided by the south-facing slopes of the Kanonkop, and the north-facing Tygerberg Hills. Being situated in the coolest wine-growing region in the country (Winkler Two category temperatures), the grapes need an extra 11–14 very beneficial days to ripen. Most of the ground is deep, heavy Hutton-type clay which maintains ground moisture, so no irrigation is needed.

Well known as a supplier of top quality grapes to the wine industry (especially Cabernet Sauvignon), it was a natural progression for Elsenberg-trained Jackie to register Bloemendal as an estate and begin to bottle a selected percentage of his crop under his own 'water lily' label.

The combination of good climate – and Jackie's technical skills, artistic flair and entertaining, extrovert character – produced a string of accolades; his wines have won numerous awards.

BEVERAGES INCLUDE:
Sauvignon Blanc, Bloemen Blanc, Merlot, Cabernet Sauvignon, and Port.

Opening times:
Weekdays: 09:00 – 17:30
Saturdays: 09:00 – 13:00
• Closed on Sundays and religious holidays.
• Cellar tours by appointment.

Bloemendal
P.O. Box 466
Durbanville
7551

Tel/Fax: (021) 96 2682

DIEMERSDAL

Diemersdal, one of the oldest farms in Durbanville, was granted to free burgher Hendrik Sneewind on 18 September 1698. Governor Simon van der Stel gave him permission to plant vegetables and sow grain. Hendrik Sneewind died in 1713 and his widow, Anna Elizabeth, remarried a year later. Her second husband was Dutch ship commander Captain Diemer.

Although it is not quite clear when the first wines were produced on the farm, there are indications that Sneewind made some. This is reflected by the inventory made by his widow after his death: there were 45 vats, some wine testers and a press vat.

The farm came into the hands of the Louw family in 1885. Since then, wine making has been the main objective, although it was not always the only reason for cultivating vines – Matthys Michaels (Tienie) Louw also had a vinegar factory in Salt River.

Today, Tienie is the fourth generation of Louws on the farm. He continues with the wine making and also sows a bit of grain. Diemersdal, situated in the shadows of the Kanonkop in the Durbanville wine area, is planted with 170 ha (420 acres) of vines. Its location is particularly suitable for making high-quality wines – especially red varieties. The vineyards are not irrigated and receive some 660 mm (23.6 in) of rain per year. All the red wines are made on the estate, and the white grapes are sold. The wines are sold on the local, as well as on the international market. The capacity of the cellar is 5 900 hl (129 782 gallons).

BEVERAGES INCLUDE:
Cabernet Sauvignon, Private Collection (Bordeaux blend), Shiraz, Pinotage, Sauvignon Blanc, and Chardonnay.

Opening Times:
Weekdays: 09:00 – 17:00
Saturdays: 09:00 – 16:00

Diemersdal Estate
P.O. Box 27
Durbanville
7551

Tel: (021) 96 3361
Fax: (021) 96 1810

M eerendal dates back to 1702,
when the farm was granted to
Jan Meerland by Governor Willem
Adriaan van der Stel. By 1712,
Meerland's widow, Maria, had
60 000 vines growing on the farm.

When the Starke family first bought
the estate in 1929, only a small vineyard existed. However, it displayed
Meerendal's potential and consequently
wheat fields were turned into vineyards in the early 1930s. Virus-free
vines,consisting of noble cultivars such
as pinotage, shiraz, cabernet sauvignon,
merlot, chardonnay and sauvignon
blanc were planted.

The high quality of grapes produced,
together with modern cellar techniques,
ensures wines of excellent quality. The
370 ha (914-acre) estate has 114 ha
(282 acres) under vines. Winemaker
Soon Potgieter produces a Shiraz and
Pinotage, both of which have won
several gold medals at the annual
Veritas Awards.

Meerendal's gracious Cape Dutch
homestead is a landmark in the
Durbanville area. Overlooking the
mountains and vineyards, the pastoral
vista is truly breathtaking. The loft above
the wine cellar, with its magnificent
150-year-old Oregon pine beams and
floors, provides an elegant setting for
sampling some of the finest Meerendal
wines. In addition to wine tastings, part
of the loft also serves as a function
room or conference centre.

BEVERAGES INCLUDE:
Sauvignon Blanc, Chardonnay,
Gewürztraminer, and Cabernet Sauvignon.

Opening Times:
Weekdays: 10:00 – 17:30
Saturdays: 10:00 – 12:30
• Closed on religious holidays.

Meerendal
P.O. Box 2
Durbanville
7550

Tel: (021) 975 1655/7
Fax: (021) 975 1655

NITIDA CELLARS

Nitida Cellars is the newest and smallest wine producer in the Durbanville area. In August 1990, Bernhard and Peta Veller bought Maasspruit, which included a tiny sheep farm right in the middle of the beautiful Kloof in the Durbanville wine valley, a bull named Boris (until he had a calf), and a magnificent ram who terrorised every ewe and human on the property.

However, 37 ha (91 acres) of Clovelly-Hutton soils on a southern slope, perfect temperature conditions, cool morning and evening mists, and light Atlantic Ocean breezes were more than any wine lover could resist. After extensive testing and analysis, new clone cabernet sauvignon and pinotage, plus smaller amounts of merlot and cabernet franc were planted in 1992 and 1993.

In 1994 Ursula and Gerhard Veller, Bernhard's parents, joined the venture, bringing with them years of experience and an appreciation for fine European wines. Their love of white cultivars and the suitability of this strain to the region inspired the planting of chardonnay, sauvignon blanc and semillon vines. So, with 12 ha (30 acres) of prime soils under vine, all that was needed was a name for the wine. 'Nitida' seemed an excellent choice, since in the past *Protea nitida* had grown wild on the farm as part of the natural *renosterveld*.

The owners, who make wines that they enjoy drinking themselves, hope that their product will live up to the name's Latin roots – *nitidus* meaning bright, shiny, healthy, refined and cultured. So far they have certainly been successful – their first release, a 1995 Sauvignon Blanc, won double gold at the 1996 Veritas Awards.

BEVERAGES INCLUDE:
Pinotage, Cabernet Sauvignon, Shiraz, Chardonnay, and a Bordeaux Blend.

Opening times:
Weekdays: 09:00 – 17:30
Saturdays: 09:00 – 13:00
• Closed on Sundays and religious holidays.
• Cellar tours by appointment.

Nitida Cellars
P.O. Box 1423
Durbanville
7551

Tel/Fax: (021) 96 1467

Founded in 1679 by Simon van der Stel, this beautiful town, the second oldest in the Cape, has not been modernised beyond recognition, but remains true to its origins.

Oak-lined streets, white-washed historical buildings, the Eerste River meandering through the heart of town, a mild climate and majestic mountain ranges have made Stellenbosch a prime destination for local and international tourists, and earned it a reputation as one of the most picturesque towns in the world.

The many friendly restaurants and pubs offer local fare, continental and exotic dishes, while sidewalk cafés and meet-and-eat venues under the oaks are always popular.

The town caters for the needs of every tourist. Accommodation ranges from self-catering bed-and-breakfast establishments to quaint cottages, guest houses and luxury hotels. Many are situated in and around town, others amid the vineyards on wine farms. Discovering Stellenbosch on foot is easy

• The Rhenish Complex (Tourist Information) also houses a toy and miniature museum.

• The VOC (Powder House) in Bloem Street was a magazine, built in 1777, taking just 6 months to complete. The bell tower was added 20 years later.

• St Mary's on the Braak is an Anglican church, still in use today, that was consecrated in 1854 by Bishop Gray.

• The Town Hall, a building in pseudo Cape style, was completed in 1941.

• Dorplane, once a picturesque neighbourhood, is today the colourful domain of the local flower sellers.

• The Village Museum encompasses nearly 5 000 m^2 (5 382 ft^2) of the oldest part of the town. Lovingly restored and furnished, the Schreuder, Bletterman, Grosvenor and Bergh houses are open to the public.

• The neo-Gothic Moederkerk (mother church) was built by the German master architect, Carl Otto Hager, in 1863.

• 149, 158 and 160/2 Dorp Street is a collection of quaint historical buildings.

• The Slave House (21-35 Herte Street) is a fine example of the houses that were built for freed slaves after their emancipation in 1834.

• The exhibits of the Stellenryk Wine Museum centre on the art of wine making and wine culture.

• Oom Samie se Winkel is a typical example of a period village shop, crammed full of old fashioned articles that delight today's customers.

For guided walks through the historical village contact:
Stellenbosch Tourist Information
36 Market Street

Tel: (021) 883 3584 / 883 9633
Fax: (021) 883 8017

ALTO WINE ESTATE

The history of Alto Wine Estate dates back as far as 1693 when it was part of the farm Groenrivier.

In 1919 it was bought by the Malan family who gave their farm the Latin name *alto*, a reference to the high altitude of the vineyards. In 1922 they made their first Alto Rouge, a blended red wine.

A sample shipment was sent to London and the response was immediate and enthusiastic – they were offered a five-year contract for regular shipments. A link was thus set up which continued over the years. With a healthy demand for the wine from overseas, it was some years before Alto Rouge was released on the local market in 1933. Again, it was an immediate success.

Today Alto Wine Estate is the home of ex-Springbok rugby prop, Hempies du Toit. Hempies has built up a sound reputation for producing world class red wines.

He calls for a 24-hour vigil at the critical stage of fermentation. In the cellar, day and night, the young wines are then tasted and tested every four hours, to ensure outstanding quality.

Among the international awards the estate has won, were the Grand Prix d'Honneurs for the 1984 Alto Cabernet Sauvignon at the prestigious International Vinexpo in Bordeaux, France; the Dave Hughes Trophy at the International Wine and Spirit Competition in England for the Best South African Red Wine for the 1986 Cabernet Sauvignon; and more recently another Vinexpo gold medal for the 1987 Alto Cabernet Sauvignon.

The estate, which sweeps up the steep side of the scenic Helderberg mountains, forms part of Stellenbosch Wine Route and visitors can taste and buy the acclaimed red wines in the rustic tasting room decorated with the antique farm implements restored by Hempies.

BEVERAGES INCLUDE:
A select range of vintages of Alto Rouge and Alto Cabernet Sauvignon available in differently sized bottles.

Opening times:
Weekdays: 09:00 – 17:00
Saturdays: 09:00 – 12:30
• Closed on religious holidays.

Alto Wine Estate
P.O. Box 15
Lynedoch
7603

Tel/Fax: (021) 881 3884

THE BERGKELDER

Touring the Bergkelder is an unforgettable experience. The famous 'cellar in the mountain' was opened in 1968 and is the home of some of the Cape's finest wines. Apart from making and marketing wines like Stellenryck, Fleur du Cap and JC le Roux, it also markets the wines of a number of other leading wine estates like Meerlust, Alto, Uitkyk, Middelvlei and Allesverloren.

The informative cellar tour serves to introduce visitors to the art of wine making. It includes a visit to the wood maturation cellar with its capacity of 25 000, 300 l (528-pint) barrels, an overview of the making of Cap Classique sparkling wine, a visit to the bottling hall and an interesting audio-visual presentation on wine making.

The Bergkelder's world class wines can be sampled in the impressive setting of the unique maturation cellar tunnelled into the slopes of the Parrot Mountain. These corridors lead to a room with beautiful vats, skillfully carved by the artist Karl Wilhelm with scenes from the wine history of the Cape. The tour ends in the Bergkelder Wine Shop with the sampling of the dessert wines.

BEVERAGES INCLUDE:

The ranges of the following wine farms:
Allesverloren, Alto, Du Cap, Fleur du Cap,
Grünberger, HC Collison, Here XVII,
Jacobsdal, JC le Roux, Kupferberger,

La Motte, Le Bonheur, L'Ormarins,
Meerendal, Meerlust, Middelvlei, Mont
Blois, Pongracz, Rietvallei, Stellenryk,
Theuniskraal, Uitkyk, and Oude Meester.

Tours are conducted daily:
Afrikaans/English: 10:00
English/German/French: 10:30
English: 15:00
Special tours arranged on request.

Tastings and sales:
Weekdays: 09:00 – 17:00
Saturdays: 09:00 – 13:00

Cellar tours (9 December to 11 January):
Weekdays: 10:00, 10:30, 11:00, 12:00, 13:00, 14:00, 15:00
Saturdays: 10:00, 10:30, 11:00, 14:00, 15:00

The Bergkelder
P.O. Box 184
Stellenbosch
7599

Tel: (021) 888 3200
Fax: (021) 886 5253

Wine shop and booking of tours
Tel: (021) 888 3016
Fax: (021) 887 9081

BEYERSKLOOF WINES

Beyerskloof Wines is a small 8 ha (20-acre) wine farm in the Koelenhof area close to Stellenbosch.

Beyers Truter (winemaker of the Kanonkop Estate) and four ardent wine lovers from Johannesburg bought the unplanted property in 1988 with the intention of making a wine of exceptional character.

Since its inception it was established that Beyerskloof would be a boutique winery. Only two wines are produced: a big, intense Cabernet Sauvignon with great maturation potential, made in very small quantities, and a lovely fruity, easy-drinking Pinotage produced in larger volumes.

The gravelly clay soils, similar to those of the great wine growing region of Bordeaux, called for cabernet sauvignon and merlot to be planted.

The first Beyerskloof wine was produced in 1989 with bought-in cabernet sauvignon grapes that adhered to Beyers' exacting standards. Minimum interference with the best quality grapes and traditional methods were utilised to produce this classic, concentrated wine. For the period 1989–1994 only this one wine, simply called Beyerskloof, was produced.

During 1995 the owners of Kanonkop, Johann and Paul Krige, also acquired shares in Beyerskloof. The next logical step for the 'Pinotage King' (as Beyers Truter is known) was to produce a pinotage – a grape variety he passionately believes has enormous under-utilised potential.

Grapes produced by surrounding farms had to comply with rigorous standards before they were included in the first Beyerskloof Pinotage launched locally and on the overseas market. Beyerskloof was awarded the State President's Award for Export Achievement in the Agro-Industrial Sector in 1996.

The visitor can enjoy the personal attention of knowledgeable staff in the cosy tasting room, which offers beautiful views of the Simonsberg and surrounding mountains.

BEVERAGES INCLUDE:
Pinotage and Cabernet Sauvignon.

Opening times:
Weekdays: 09:00 – 16:30
• Please phone to confirm hours on Saturdays.

Beyerskloof Wines
P.O. Box 107
Koelenhof
7605

Tel: (021) 882 2135
Fax: (021) 882 2683

BLAAUWKLIPPEN

Blaauwklippen vineyards are situated on prime west- and south-facing locations where the remarkable altitude variation allows for the production of different styles of handmade wines. These wines are natural blends created by the mountain and the valley. You can taste the effect – even the pure varietal wines are blends of light and heavy, full and supple, soft and spicy.

Founded over 300 years ago, Blaauwklippen has seen generations pass and lifestyles come and go. Today, a rare historical collection of furniture, carriages and vintage cars can be admired at Blaauwklippen and there is an extensive range of homemade jams, preserves, salamis and more to whet your appetite.

BEVERAGES INCLUDE:
Chardonnay, Chardonnay/Semillon, Sauvignon Blanc, Sociable White, Rhine Riesling, White Landau, Muscat Ottonel, Special Late Vintage, Cabernet Sauvignon, Zinfandel, Shiraz, Pinot Noir, Red Landau, Sociable Dry Red, and Port.

Opening times:
Weekdays: 09:00 – 17:00
Saturdays: 09:00 – 13:00

• Coachman's Lunch:
In summer (1 October – 30 April):
12:00 – 14:30
In winter (1 May – 30 September):
12:00 – 14:30

• Coach rides by horse-drawn carriage: Mondays to Fridays (1 October – Easter) at 10:00, 12:00, 14:00 and 15:45, weather permitting.

Cellar Tours:
Weekdays: 11:00, 15:00
Saturdays: 11:00
• Guided tours throughout the day from 1 December to 31 January, according to demand.

Blaauwklippen
P.O. Box 54
Stellenbosch
7599

Tel: (021) 880 0133
Fax: (021) 880 0136

DELAIRE

Delaire, the 'vineyard in the sky', is small but beautifully situated on the Helshoogte Mountain Pass and has views that will take your breath away. This 19 ha (47-acre) vineyard experiences altitude variations which range from approximately 300 to 500 m (984 to 1 640 ft) above sea level.

Winemaker Bruwer Raats maintains that nature is the vineyards' partner. He believes that wine is made first in the vineyard; after that the human art form of wine making requires a good dash of common sense, a keen sense of taste and colour and a love of wine, combined with a responsive gut feel.

Bruwer aims for red wines that are big in structure, with soft tannins and elegance, while his white wines must capture the freshness of the harvest.

The terroir, the long cool winters, and the slow ripening season means that this estate has the material for world-class wines. However, in order to pick at optimum ripeness in the Banhoek Valley, a certain amount of courage is called for – the estate may have to wait for up to three weeks after their Stellenbosch neighbours have picked, for their grapes to ripen – in the words of Bruwer, "the suspense is killing!".

Since 1995, when Delaire was acquired by a division of Middlesex Holdings PLC, it has been experiencing a centennial renaissance, with extensive investment in the cellar, the farm and its staff. The UK directors, led by

Masoud Alikhani, who has a passion for wine and a great love for this country, are proud of their first investment in South Africa.

The Green Door Restaurant is perfectly placed for guests to enjoy leisurely meals and sip delicious wines, while revelling in the glory of the panorama that stretches from sunrise to sunset.

A stay at one of the mountain lodges provides the ideal setting for experiencing, at first hand, the grape harvest, pruning of the vines and the art of making fine wines.

BEVERAGES INCLUDE:
Sauvignon Blanc, Weisser Riesling, Late Harvest, Chardonnay, and Joie de L'Air (sparkling wine from chardonnay grapes). Red wines are Cabernet Sauvignon, Pinotage, and a limited edition of Merlot Cabernet Sauvignon in 1.5 l (2-pint) magnums.

Opening times:
Mondays to Saturdays: 10:00 – 17:00
• Open on Sundays in season.

Delaire
P.O. Box 3058
Stellenbosch
7602

Tel: (021) 885 1756
Fax: (021) 885 1270

STELLENBOSCH   43

Delheim lies on the slopes of the Simonsberg Mountain, overlooking Cape Town and with a splendid view of Table Mountain.

The original farm, Driesprongh (three jumps) was founded in 1699. It was purchased by Hans Hoheisen in 1938, who planted the first vines in 1940. Delheim, meaning 'Deli's home' (after Hans' wife) was established in 1972 by Mr Hoheisen and vintner, Spatz Sperling.

Today it comprises three farms: Driesprongh, Vera Cruz and Klapmuts. Driesprongh, which is home to Delheim's cellar, tasting and sales facilities, spans the slopes of the Simonsberg between 300 to 400 m (984 to 1 312 ft) above sea level. The cool climate, hutton-type soils and annual average rainfall of 500 mm (19.7 in) which prevail here favour the growing of white wine varieties.

Vera Cruz and Klapmuts, lie 5 km (3 miles) lower down the valley and produce the fuller bodied red wines which require a drier, warmer climate. The south-facing vineyards, rising gradually from 200 to 355 m (656 to 1 165 ft), are noted for their loamy, sandy soils. Annual rainfall is around 3 per cent lower than on Driesprongh. The vineyards also enjoy 10 to 12 days more sunshine, making this one of the top red wine farms in the area.

BEVERAGES INCLUDE:

Heerenwijn, Semillon, Sauvignon Blanc, Chardonnay, Chenin Blanc, Grandesse, Gewürztraminer, Pinotage Rosé, Dry Red, Merlot, Shiraz, Cabernet Sauvignon, Grand Reserve, Goldspatz Stein, Spatzendreck Late Harvest, Special Late Harvest, Edelspatz Noble Late Harvest, Red and White grape juice.

Opening times: (1 November to 31 March)
Weekdays: 08:30 – 17:00
Saturdays: 09:00 – 15:00
Sundays: 11:30 – 15:00
• Closed on Christmas Day.
• Summer lunches (1 October – 30 April)
Mondays to Saturdays: 12:00 – 14:30
(1 November to 28 February)
Sundays: 12:00 – 14:30
• Winter lunches (1 May – 30 September)
Mondays to Saturdays: 12:00 – 14:30
Booking is essential for groups.

Cellar tours: *(1 October to 30 April)*
Weekdays: 10:30 and 14:30
(1 May to 30 September)
Weekdays: 14:30
Saturdays: 10:30 (throughout the year)

Delheim Wines
P.O. Box 10
Koelenhof
7605

Tel: (021) 882 2033
Fax: (021) 882 2036
Restaurant Tel: (021) 882 2297
Email: delheim@iafrica.com

GOEDE HOOP

G oede Hoop wine estate is situated off the old road that connected the towns of Stellenbosch and Kuilsriver, deep in the valley known as the Bottelary Kloof.

The old farmhouse, rich in atmosphere, was built in 1880. In 1928 the Bestbier family purchased the wine estate and today Pieter Bestbier is its third-generation winemaker.

The 120 ha (296-acre) estate is situated on the slopes of the valley and about 80 ha (197 acres) have been planted with vines facing mainly north and northwest. 350 m (1 148 ft) separate the lowest and highest vineyards and meso-climates abound.

Temperature and rainfall differences between the individual vineyards are considerable. Also, the horse-shoe shape of the vineyards ensures the right hours of sunshine for every variety. These conditions – the temperate climate, as well as quality of the soil – are ideal for producing wines of excellence.

The vineyards are not irrigated as rainfall is sufficient at 600–900 mm (23–35 in) per annum.

BEVERAGES INCLUDE:
Sauvignon Blanc, Vin Blanc, Cabernet Sauvignon, and Vintage Rouge.

• Tasting and sales by appointment only.

Goede Hoop
P.O. Box 25
Kuilsriver
7580

Tel: (021) 903 6286
Fax: (021) 906 1553

HARTENBERG

Hartenberg Estate is located to the north-west of Stellenbosch. The cultivation of grapes and the making of wines have been part of the Hartenberg story for over 300 years. Since the days when a Frenchman named L'Estreux first planted vines here, the never-ending cycle has continued, though the farm has passed through many hands.

Since 1987, it has been owned and managed by the MacKenzie family, who have undertaken a major replanting and development programme to ensure that the wines of Hartenberg Estate remain amongst the most sought-after. Winemaker Carl Schultz, who joined the estate in 1993, has set about redefining the Hartenberg style.

With a wide range of soil types, Hartenberg Estate is ideally suited for the cultivation of an equally broad range of varieties. The soils and climate are particularly suitable for reds like Shiraz, Cabernet Sauvignon and Merlot. But Hartenberg is also noted for its excellent white varietal wines, including Chardonnay, Sauvignon Blanc and Weisser Riesling, as well as a number of fruity, flavourful blended wines.

Hartenberg's reds are matured for up to 18 months in either French or American oak barrels, and are generally not released until at least four years after vintage.

Visitors are warmly welcomed at Hartenberg Estate throughout the year. Taste the wines and enjoy a vintner's lunch under the trees on the terrace in summer, or a homemade soup in the tasting room by a warming fire in winter. Booking for lunch is advisable.

BEVERAGES INCLUDE:
Chatillon, Sauvignon Blanc, Weisser Riesling, L'Estreux (Gewürztraminer Special Late Harvest), Chardonnay, Cabernet Sauvignon Shiraz, Zinfandel (red), Pontac (limited volume red wine), Cabernet Sauvignon, Merlot, Shiraz, and Bin wines in dry, semi-sweet, rosé and red.

Opening times:
Weekdays: 09:00 – 17:00
Saturdays: 09:00 – 14:00
• Lunches served Mondays to Saturdays from 12:00 – 14:00.

Hartenberg Estate
P.O. Box 69
Koelenhof
7605

Tel: (021) 882 2541
Fax: (021) 882 2153

HAZENDAL

Hazendal Wine Estate is one of the oldest and most beautiful estates in the area. Christoffel Hazenwinkel, its first owner, was granted the estate by Adriaan van der Stel in 1704. Thereafter it was purchased by Joost Reynard van As. In 1831 the farm changed hands yet again. Its new owner was Izaak Daniel Bosman, whose children cultivated these beautiful winelands for five flourishing generations.

Finally, in 1994, Russian-born entrepreneur Dr Mark Voloshin, chairman of the international Marvol Group, showed his confidence in the 'new' South Africa by investing in the natural and human resources of the estate, whose rich, moist and fertile soils produce the flavourful wines of Hazendal.

Winemaker Hein Hesebeck gives careful attention to the cultivation of superb grapes. He has personally directed the thorough replanting of the vineyards which will eventually produce 800 tons of grapes per vintage. No irrigation is used and wine is made in the natural way. Technology is kept to a minimum and always balanced with natural principles. The expertise of Hein, one of the region's acclaimed wine masters, combines with the wealth of natural resources to produce quality red and white wines.

The Manor House, a well-established national monument, is currently under reconstruction to retain the historic features of Hazendal. The baroque gable, yellowwood ceilings and panelling are being restored. The main homestead will be converted into a museum, also acting as an entrance to a hotel, to be developed later. The modern wine cellar will co-exist with the original wine cellar which is now developed into a wine tasting centre. An underground barrel fermentation cellar will be included.

BEVERAGES INCLUDE:
Sauvignon Blanc, Chardonnay (fermented in American oak), Chenin Blanc (dry), Chenin Blanc (fermented in American oak), Chenin Blanc Special Late Harvest, and Shiraz/Cabernet Sauvignon.

Sales and tastings:
Weekdays: 09:00 – 17:00
Saturdays: 09:30 – 15:00
Sundays: 10:00 – 15:00

Hazendal Wine Estate
P.O. Box 336
Stellenbosch
7600

Tel: (021) 903 5034/5
Fax: (021) 903 0057

Hoopenburg Wine Farm, in the Muldersvlei area near the town of Stellenbosch, is one of the Cape's foremost boutique wineries. It has gained widespread recognition since the release of its first wines in 1992.

The energetic team behind the beautiful Hoopenburg Wine Farm is the Gouws family: Ernst, his wife Gwenda and their three children. Ernst co-owns Hoopenburg with a German partner and has been applying years of experience to produce a fine range of wines.

The grapes come from the 22 ha (54 acres) of vineyards on Hoopenburg, but Ernst also buys grapes from the quality Wine of Origin Stellenbosch and Coastal Region areas.

Hoopenburg has an annual production of some 17 000 cases and its success is due to the continuous quality of its products. So far, seven Hoopenburg wines have come out tops at panel tastings of South Africa's two largest commercial wine clubs, while the 1993, 1994 and 1995 Chardonnay were selected for the prestigious Nederburg Wine Auction. The 1996 Chardonnay was placed third out of 23 at the competition of the Chardonnay du Monde 1997 in Beaune, France.

The stylish green-and-crimson labels which grace the bottles depict two little steenbokkies (small indigenous buck) in silhouette, etched in gold against a black background, bestowing a very South African character.

The Hoopenburg range of wines are sold in selected restaurants and outlets countrywide and are also exported to various countries in Europe. However, a large part of the sales occurs through postal orders and on the farm, where wine enthusiasts are welcomed with true Boland hospitality by real wine people.

BEVERAGES INCLUDE:
Cabernet Sauvignon, Merlot, Pinot Noir, Chardonnay, and Sauvignon Blanc.

Opening times:
Weekdays: 09:00 – 17:00
Saturdays: 09:00 – 13:00

Hoopenburg Wine Farm
P.O. Box 1233
Stellenbosch
7599

Tel: (021) 884 4221/2
Fax: (021) 884 4904

JORDAN WINERY

From the Jordan hillside vineyards, which stretch up the Stellenbosch Kloof and over the Bottelary Hills, one has a spectacular, panoramic view of Cape Town, Table Mountain, False Bay and historic Stellenbosch. After the 134 ha (331-acre) property was purchased by Ted and Sheelagh Jordan in 1982, it was decided to plant only virus-free classic varieties, and innovative canopy management techniques were used to produce quality grapes with intense flavours.

Rather than having to buy in grapes from other growers, or being forced to make wine from young vineyards, the Jordans decided to wait until their vineyards had reached maturity before harvesting. On tasting Jordan wines, it is evident that their patient wait has paid off.

Gary and Kathy Jordan are the Cape's very first husband-and-wife wine making and viticultural team. With their strong backgrounds in geology and economics respectively, as well as studies in oenology at the University of California, the new generation Jordans have designed and built an attractive state-of-the-art winery, bringing a new-world touch to a farm with a 300-year history of grape growing.

A serious commitment to quality means that the grapes are harvested at optimum ripeness to ensure well-structured wines with a complex concentration of fruit and flavours.

BEVERAGES INCLUDE:
Sauvignon Blanc, Chameleon (White), Chardonnay, Blanc Fumé, Rhine Riesling, Chenin Blanc (Barrel Reserve), Cabernet Sauvignon, Merlot, and Chameleon (Red).

Opening times:
Weekdays: 10:00 – 16:30
Saturdays:
09:30 – 14:30 (November – April)
09:30 – 12:30 (May – October)

Jordan Winery
P.O. Box 12592
Die Boord
Stellenbosch
7613

Tel: (021) 881 3441
Fax: (021) 881 3426

LANZERAC

Historic Lanzerac is a 300-year-old wine estate surrounded by beautiful vineyards and spectacular views. Its history dates back to 1692, when Governor Simon van der Stel granted part of a considerable tract of land to Isaac Schrijver, who named the farm Schoongezicht and planted vineyards.

The farm changed hands a number of times and, in 1811, it was transferred to Coenraad Johannes Fick. The cellar he built has been dated to 1815 and the U-shaped homestead to 1830.

In 1914 Schoongezicht was bought by Elizabeth Katherina English, who changed the name of the farm to Lanzerac and bottled the first Lanzerac wine from grapes grown on her land.

After her death in 1929 the farm was bought by Johannes Tribbelhorn, who became a member of the Cape Quality Wine Growers' Association and, by 1936, had established what was then one of the most modern wine cellars in the Cape.

Angus Buchanan bought the farm in 1941 and bottled his first wines in 1947, earning numerous prizes over the next decade. He sold the farm in 1958 to David and Graham Rawdon, who converted the homestead and outbuildings into a luxury hotel.

Stellenbosch Farmers' Winery purchased the Lanzerac trademark in 1958, taking over the management of the vineyards and producing Pinotage, as well as Lanzerac Rosé.

In the late 1970's the farm stopped cultivating vineyards. The Rawdons sold Lanzerac to a consortium in 1988, and in 1991 it was acquired by Cape businessman Christo Wiese and his family.

It has long since been the dream of the owner, Christo Wiese, to once again produce wine on his estate. Vineyards were planted in 1992 and Wynand Hamman (winemaker) and Vriesenhof's Jan 'Boland' Coetzee (consultant) were appointed to ensure that Lanzerac regains its status as one of the country's leading wine-producing farms.

BEVERAGES INCLUDE:
Cabernet Sauvignon, Merlot, Chardonnay.

Opening times:
Mondays to Saturdays: 10:00 – 16:00
• Cellar tours by appointment only.

Lanzerac Manor and Winery
P.O. Box 4
Stellenbosch
7599

Tel: (021) 887 1132
Fax: (021) 887 2310

Winery:
Tel: (021) 886 5641
Fax: (021) 887 6998

L'AVENIR

L'Avenir is one of the new breed of small wine estates dedicated to the growing and production of fine wines on an international level. In French *l'avenir* means future, in Stellenbosch it is a representation of the present.

L'Avenir is a small 70 ha (173-acre) estate, with 45 ha (111 acres) planted to grape vines. This ensures total control from the vines to the bottle and beyond – only estate-grown grapes are pressed, matured and bottled here.

Nestled in the foothills of the Simonsberg Mountain the vineyards are a grower's dream: controllable in size and offering various slopes and exposures for quality. There is both a northern and southern to south-western exposure with afternoon breezes from False Bay cooling the grapes and allowing for an evening of respite after the day's heat.

The vineyards are dry-farmed with rich soils that absorb the winter rains. Grapes are picked for ripeness and taste flavours. Ageing takes place in small French oak barrels, constantly renewed, which form part of the integration of flavours and balance.

The farm's production, amounting to some 20 000 cases, is roughly divided between reds and whites. The red wines are from merlot, cabernet and pinotage, while whites come mostly from chardonnay, sauvignon and chenin. L'Avenir's wines are exported to many parts of the world and have been award-winners locally, at the Chardonnay du Monde in France, and the International Wine and Spirits Competition in London.

L'Avenir Wine Estate offers dramatic views of the beauty of the Cape. A luxurious guest house with a pool and nine *en-suite* bedrooms is located on the farm. Stroll through the vineyards or laze by the pond while savouring the rich, fruity wines – a warm welcome awaits you.

BEVERAGES INCLUDE:
White wines are Mon Blanc, Sauvignon Blanc, Chardonnay, Chenin Blanc, and Vin d'Estrelle. Red wines consist of the L'Ami Simon vintages, Cabernet Sauvignon, and Merlot/Cabernet Private Bin.

Opening times:
Weekdays: 10:00 – 17:00
Saturdays: 10:00 – 16:00

L'Avenir Estate
P.O. Box 1135
Stellenbosch
7599

Tel: (021) 889 5001
Fax: (021) 889 7313

LE BONHEUR

The history of this estate stretches back to 1790 when it was founded by a member of the De Villiers clan, a family of wine farmers near La Rochelle, France. Due to the persecution of the Protestant faith they left for Holland.

When the directors of the Dutch East India Company decided that the agricultural potential of the Cape colony demanded the import of farmers, the three De Villiers' brothers were among the hopeful pioneers to be accepted. They reached the Cape in 1689 and were granted land around Franschhoek.

They were a large family. The three brothers had 24 children between them and they gradually acquired considerably more property. The farm Nattevallei (wet valley) was bought by Abraham de Villiers in 1770. After his father's death, Abraham Pieter sold a portion of this farm to his brother Jacob Izaak in 1820, who named it Weltevreden (satisfied).

Jacob Izaak de Villiers made wine on Weltevreden until his death, whereafter his widow sold the farm. It has since had various owners.

When Michael Woodhead acquired the estate in 1972, the vineyards were in bad condition and no wine had been produced for 50 years. Michael started a complete programme to build up the soil and re-plant the vineyards. The Bergkelder took over the farm from Michael Woodhead during the early nineties.

Today the 163 ha (403-acre) wine estate has about 60 ha (149 acres) under vineyards and is carefully controlled by winemaker Sakkie Kotze. The Cabernet Sauvignon has won several Veritas gold medals in the past, and is regularly selected for South African Airways prestigious wine list.

The manor house has been restored and the estate is open for wine tastings and sales.

BEVERAGES INCLUDE:
Le Bonheur Blanc Fumé, Le Bonheur Chardonnay, Le Bonheur Prima, and Le Bonheur Cabernet Sauvignon.

Opening times:
Weekdays: 09:00 – 17:00
Saturdays: 09:00 – 12:30
• Closed on Sundays and religious holidays.

Le Bonheur
P.O. Box 56
Klapmuts
7625

Tel: (021) 875 5478
Fax: (021) 875 5624

L'EMIGRÉ

Half-hidden in the shade of the old oak and nut trees, nestled against the eastern foothills of the Stellenbosch-kloof and with its vineyards stretching over to the Bottelary, lies a small gem of the old Cape Dutch tradition. L'Emigré is owned and run by the Gentis family. Tiny and Cheryl handle the bottling and guest-cottages, Marc and Chimene the export and finances, Victor is the expert in viticulture, and Frans and Emile are responsible for the wine making and building.

Although still largely a co-op grape producer, the initiative to make wine was taken by Frans after retiring from the board of Welmoed Co-op, where he had served as director for 28 years (13 years of which as chairman). A versatile man, he is probably the last of the real, old, Cape Dutch builders, who, like the generations before him, undertakes all projects with his own workers.

L'Emigré started producing wine in 1994, even though the cellar had not been completed yet.

Tiny and Frans, both of whom are of immigrant stock, wanted to portray this fact on their wine labels but couldn't quite make it work. Then it struck them that the grapevine itself was an immigrant from the Middle East, and Tiny came up with the elegant L'Emigré design. Son Victor brought in his marketing expertise, and the outstanding azure design took shape under his guidance.

The talent and creativity of the Gentis family has produced some superb wines, bottled and labelled in such a manner that the end-product is of the highest quality.

Its beautiful location and heritage-style buildings make L'Emigré well worth a visit.

BEVERAGES INCLUDE:
Cabernet Sauvignon, a Bordeaux Blend, Shiraz, Pinotage, Sauvignon Blanc, Chardonnay, a sweet natural wine, a Muscat dessert wine, and a vintage port.

• The tasting room is open for one week at Easter, a fortnight at Christmas and every Saturday from 09:00 – 17:00.

L'Emigré
P.O. Box 14
Vlottenburg
7604

Tel: (021) 881 3702/3
Fax: (021) 881 3030

On the cool slopes of the Devon Valley and the Papegaaiberg, the ·Smit family has been producing wine and brandy for the past century.

Stefan Smit, the owner and cellar master of Louiesenhof, studied oenology at Weinsberg, the oldest wine institute in Germany, for four years. Here he became intensely aware of the sensitivity of ecology, thus Louiesenhof's wines are produced with a high consciousness of nature.

The wide range of soils on slopes at different altitudes, enabled Stefan and a team of viticultural experts to establish the most suitable cultivars in ideal micro-climates. In the cellar the wine is merely guided, resulting in a product that carries the distinctive character of it's origin.

Louiesenhof is a founding member of the South African Port Producers Association. For their port, Louiesenhof uses only tinta barocca grapes picked at a low sugar for flavour retention. Fermentation was stopped with 100 per cent brandy that was barrel-aged for 3 years in the Limousine barrels and afterwards barrel-aged for 2,5 years. Very dry and extremely elegant, Louiesenhof Marbonne Brandy is made from specially selected columbar and ugni blanc vineyards in Stellenbosch and is aged in limousine oak casks. This potstill – 38 per cent vol. brandy – is a real connoisseur's sipping brandy.

Louiesenhof has five newly renovated, free-standing Victorian cottages, surrounded by lawns, orchards and vineyards and a beautiful view of the Simonsberg.

BEVERAGES INCLUDE:
Louiesenhof Pinot Gris, Louiesenhof Chenin Blanc, Premier Collection Chardonnay 1997, Louiesenhof Red, Merlot, Shiraz, Cabernet Sauvignon, Premier Collection Pinotage, Louiesenhof Port, and Louiesenhof Marbonne Brandy.

Opening times:
(1 September – 31 May)
Mondays to Saturdays: 09:00 – 17:00
Sundays: 11:00 – 17:00
(1 June – 31 August)
Mondays to Fridays: 09:00 – 17:00
Saturdays: 09:00 – 13:00
• Bistro lunches and picnics offered.

Louiesenhof
P.O. Box 2013
Stellenbosch
7601

Tel/Fax: (021) 889 7309
or 882 2632

LOUISVALE

Louisvale is situated in the tranquil Devon Valley. The farm, with its exquisite views over Stellenbosch, measures 17 ha (42 acres) in extent and benefits from an ideal meso-climate of rich soils and cooling coastal winds.

The Louisvale homestead was built according to plans by famed architect Sir Herbert Baker. The farm is managed and operated by the energetic proprietors, Hans Froehling and Leon Stemmet. Their hands-on approach and meticulous attention to detail ensure that the farm operates to the same standards of excellence that they demand of their wines.

The cellar, built in 1990, comprises both a pressing and fermentation cellar and a specially designed barrel maturation cellar. These facilities are tailored to the production of top quality wines.

The jewel in Louisvale's crown is their Chardonnay. Acclaimed both nationally and internationally, the wine is made exclusively from grapes grown on Louisvale farm, which is planted to both Californian- and French-clone chardonnay. The Louisvale red wines, a Merlot and a Cabernet Sauvignon, are vinified from grapes selected from neighbouring farms. Intent on keeping abreast of both local and international tastes, Louisvale have extended their repertoire. Louisvale Chavant is a lighter Chardonnay, of which the farm produces both a lightly wooded and an unwooded variety. These are complemented by two classic, blended wines – a Sauvignon Blanc Chardonnay and a red blend of Cabernet Sauvignon, Merlot and Cabernet Franc – all of which bring a broad spectrum of quality and taste to Louisvale wine lovers.

Hans and Leon do not only produce award-winning wines, but are also champion breeders of Miniature Schnauzers and Great Danes. This partnership, along with one of the country's top winemakers, forms the core of professionalism behind Louisvale farm.

BEVERAGES INCLUDE:
Louisvale Chardonnay, Merlot, Louisvale Chavant, Sauvignon Blanc, Chardonnay, and LV Cabernet Sauvignon.

Opening times:
Weekdays: 10:00 – 17:00
Saturdays: 10:00 – 13:00

Louisvale Farm
P.O. Box 542
Stellenbosch
7599

Tel: (021) 882 2422
Fax: (021) 882 2633

MIDDELVLEI

Middelvlei, shaped like a horse-shoe, is situated on the outskirts of Stellenbosch and spreads its vineyards along the northern slopes of Papegaaiberg – the Stellenbosch mountain where Governor Simon van der Stel used to shoot at wooden parrots for target practice.

The suburbs of Stellenbosch have crept around the mountains, virtually up to the gate of this wine estate.

The present owner is Stiljan Momberg, whose family has been on Middelvlei for generations. Since 1992, the wine farm has been managed by Stiljan's sons, Tinnie and Ben. Tinnie is the new winemaker and, like his father, believes in traditional methods of wine making – such as fermentation in open tanks. Ben is responsible for Middelvlei's meticulously tended vineyards. These were the first vineyards to have tell-tale rose bushes heading the rows of vines, as in France, to give early warning of possible vine diseases.

Soil and climate, careful farming, modest facilities and progressive know-how have made Middelvlei a foremost red wine producer. The estate forms part of the Stellenbosch Wine Route and the tasting centre is a pleasing traditional building looking across a dam.

Apart from being enthusiastic wine lovers, the Mombergs are also animal lovers and around the tasting room you will find Kolbroock pigs, squirrels, buck, tortoise, a crow, and the two donkeys, Port and Jeripico.

Picnic baskets are available from the beginning of December during the summer months.

BEVERAGES INCLUDE:
Cabernet Sauvignon, Shiraz, a Pinotage/ Merlot blend, Pinotage, and Chardonnay.

Opening times:
Weekdays: 09:00 – 12:00 / 13:30 – 16:30
Saturdays: 09:00 – 12:00

Middelvlei
P.O. Box 66
Stellenbosch
7600

Tel: (021) 883 2565
Fax: (021) 883 9646

Originally granted in 1692, Morgenhof has had many owners in its time but none quite as dynamic as Alain and Anne Huchon.

The Huchons are steeped in cognac, definitely not through consumption but certainly through history. Anne Cointreau-Huchon can trace her family tree back to 1210, when the family was already in the business. The Huchons brought with them tremendous knowledge and expertise flowing from their family involvement in great cognacs such as Frapin, Chateau Paulet and world-famous liqueurs.

Following their purchase of the 153 ha (378-acre) Morgenhof farm, the Huchons bought the adjoining properties of Merom and Harmony to re-establish the farm as it was 300 years ago. Morgenhof now measures some 213 ha (526 acres) in extent and the current 57 ha (141 acres) of vine will gradually be increased to about 80 ha (198 acres).

Although Morgenhof boasted a modern cellar in 1993, this has been improved with the building of an underground maturation cellar to give the talented winemaker, Jean Daneel, the tools to make the best quality wine. Among a number of other developments, the very best of wine presses has been installed to handle the grapes as gently as possible.

It is a Morgenhof policy to replant some 5–7 ha (12–17 acres) of vineyard annually to ensure continuous replacement of the most modern virus-free material. Morgenhof is very much a team effort, ably lead by Anne Cointreau-Huchon as chairman, Alain Huchon as managing director and Jean Daneel as cellar master, in charge of all production and vineyards. Indulge yourself in a little wine tasting at Morgenhof and pause awhile longer to enjoy the culinary delights that are served in the form of a light luncheon, all year round.

BEVERAGES INCLUDE:
Cabernet Sauvignon, Merlot, Sauvignon Blanc, Chardonnay, Rhine Riesling, Dry Red, Port, and Cap Classique.

Opening times:
Weekdays: 09:00 – 16:30
Saturdays and Sundays: 10:00 – 15:00 (September – May)
• Lunches served from 12:00 – 14:30 on Mondays, Saturdays and Sundays (September – May).
• Light lunches served all year round.

Morgenhof
P.O. Box 365
Stellenbosch
7599

Tel: (021) 889 5510
Fax: (021) 889 5266

MURATIE

Muratie is believed to be one of the oldest privately owned wine estates in South Africa, and visiting it is akin to stepping into a time warp. The old homestead with its neo-classical façade and gable is matched by the interior furnishings and decor which have remained untouched for almost a century. The original cement fermentation tanks in the 200-year-old gabled cellar are still in use today, and outside, the stoep is strewn with old wine making equipment, retired from use only recently.

Artist George Canitz and his daughter Annemarie bought the rundown land in 1925 and set about restoring the homestead and the farm. Not being a winemaker, George Canitz relied heavily on the advice of his good friend, Professor Abraham Perold, the 'father of Pinotage', who believed that the rich red Hutton soils and climate at Muratie were ideal for red wines. When George Canitz died in 1959 his daughter, Annemarie, took over the running of the farm. When she was convinced that Ronnie Melck would honour the Muratie tradition she sold him the farm in 1988.

In keeping with the Muratie red wine tradition, Ronnie Melck replanted a third of the estate's older vines to noble red cultivars, predominantly pinot noir, cabernet sauvignon and merlot.

In 1995, the Muratie Estate Cabernet Sauvignon won the Roberto Moni trophy for the best bottled red wine at the SA National Young Wine Show and the Jan Smuts trophy for the champion wine that year.

Ronnie Melck, whose passion for uplifting Muratie was enormous, passed away in September of the same year. Fortuitously, his widow Annetjie and sons Rijk and Anton share his vision, and out of respect and love for him carry forward his dream and legacy.

BEVERAGES INCLUDE:
Only red wines, like Pinot Noir, Merlot, Cabernet Sauvignon, Ansela (Cabernet Sauvignon/Merlot), and Muratie Port.

Opening times:
Mondays – Tuesdays: 09:00 – 17:00
Fridays: 09:00 – 16:00
Saturdays: 09:00 – 15:00
Public holidays: 09:00 – 15:00

Muratie Estate
P.O. Box 133
Koelonhof
7605

Tel: (021) 882 2330
Fax: (021) 882 2790

NEETHLINGSHOF ESTATE

In 1692 a German immigrant, Barend Lubbe, began farming in the Bottelary hills. He named the farm De Wolwedans (dance of the wolves) – derived from the packs of jackals that roamed the countryside.

After Lubbe, the farm belonged to the Marais family, who were responsible for the building of the wine cellar and the manor house. Their son-in-law, Marthinus Neethling, earned himself the nickname Lord Neethling, because of his flamboyant character – and the farm was renamed Neethlingshof.

The farm belonged to the Louw family for the next 100 years. It passed from generation to generation, each one adding to its reputation as producing some of the Cape's finest wines.

In 1985, Hans-Joachim Schreiber, an international banker and financier, bought Neethlingshof Estate and set about major renovations and improvements as well as an extensive vineyard replanting programme. Schalk van der Westhuizen, who has lived on the farm all his life, was responsible for the initial replanting programme, but came back to the cellar in 1993 to produce the quality wines for which Neethlingshof is so well known.

At the 1996 SA Championship Wine show, Schalk's Weisser Riesling Noble Late Harvest (botrytis), was awarded the trophy as the South African National Champion for a record seventh year! At the 1996 Veritas Awards,

Neethlingshof received a total of 16 awards, including 5 gold medals. On the international front it is no different, indicating that the wines from this estate appeal to palates around the world. Neethlingshof's Weisser Riesling Noble Late Harvest 1995, was awarded the prestigious blue gold medal at the 1996 Top 100 International Wine Show in Sydney, Australia.

Neethlingshof offers wine tastings, cellar tours and estate tours.

BEVERAGES INCLUDE:
A full range of white and red wines, such as Neethlingshoffer (a blend of Sauvignon Blanc, Cape Riesling and Weisser Riesling), Gewürztraminer, and Neethlingsrood (a blend of Cabernet Sauvignon and Shiraz).

Opening times:
Weekdays: 09:00 – 17:00
Saturdays and Sundays: 10:00 – 16:00
• Cellar tours by appointment only.
• Closed Good Friday and Christmas Day.
• Estate tours are available from
1 November to 15 April every year.

Neethlingshof Estate
P.O. Box 104
Stellenbosch
7599

Tel: (021) 883 8988
Fax: (021) 883 8941/883 8975

OUDE LIBERTAS

The presence of Adam Tas, one of the original owners of the estate, can still be sensed in the surroundings and atmosphere of Oude Libertas.

Adam Tas remains a memorable character, not least for the leading role he played in exposing the corruption of Governor Willem Adriaan van der Stel which led to his imprisonment. After his release a year later, van der Stel and other important officials were dismissed from their posts. Celebrating his new-found freedom with characteristic conviviality and free-flowing wine, Adam Tas named his farm Libertas. Many years later, the name Oude Libertas still echoes with the sounds of freedom, success and good cheer.

Today, Oude Libertas is the home of the Stellenbosch Farmer's Winery – one of the biggest wineries in the world which has, in the past decades, produced wines that are enjoyed all over the world.

The modern spaciousness of the building and the ambience of its magnificent surroundings have made it the centre of elegant entertainment in the Cape winelands. It houses not only a magnificent vinotheque, restaurant, conference centre and amphitheatre, but also one of the world's most respected wine academies.

BEVERAGES INCLUDE:
A full range of white wines, sparkling wines like Grand Mousseaux, port, sherry, brandy, whiskey, fruit juices, and liqueurs.

Opening times:
Monday – Thursday: 08:15 – 17:00
Friday: 08:15 – 16:00
Saturday: 10:00 – 13:00
• Restaurant open for lunches Mondays to Fridays, and dinners Mondays to Saturdays.

Oude Libertas
P.O. Box 46
Stellenbosch
7599

Tel: (021) 808 7569/99
Fax: (021) 887 2506/886 4568
Special functions: (021) 808 7429
Email: vandreve@iafrica.com

RUST EN VREDE

Established in 1694, historical Rust en Vrede and its wine cellar now belongs to the Engelbrecht family.

The present proprietor, Mr. Jannie Engelbrecht, bought the small and run-down estate in 1978 and dedicated himself to restoring it to its former splendour. A family business, and managed by people to whom top quality and respect for tradition are constant priorities, Rust en Vrede became an immediate success, since its very first vintage in 1979.

Classic cultivars grown on the estate include cabernet sauvignon, shiraz, merlot and tinta barocca. A distinctive blend is also made using only grapes of superior quality from each harvest – a wine which truly embodies the uniqueness of the estate and is simply known as Rust en Vrede Estate Wine.

In 1991, Rust en Vrede joined the international market and was awarded the coveted National Award For Export Achievement in 1994. Some 50 per cent of its total production is exported to 17 different countries. At the 1993 Nobel Peace Awards held in Oslo, the Rust en Vrede 1989 Merlot was served during the prestigious dinner. Rust en Vrede's wines have graced the dinner tables of state functions and other note-worthy events. Furthermore, the wines are found on the wine lists of South Africa's most prestigious restaurants and international airlines.

Rust en Vrede is one of the Cape's premium red wine estates with 30 ha (74 acres) of vineyard. The unique underground cellar was the first of its kind in South Africa for a privately owned estate.

The original house, dating back to circa 1780, is today known as the Jonkershuis. During the same period, a wine cellar was erected. The manor house was built around 1790, although the date on the gable states 1825, indicating the year in which the gable was restored after a fire. All three historical buildings are fine examples of the Cape Dutch architectural era (1780 until 1825).

BEVERAGES INCLUDE:
Rust en Vrede Estate Wine.

Opening times:
Weekdays: 08:30 – 16:30
Saturdays: 09:30 – 13:00

Rust en Vrede Wine Estate
P.O. Box 473
Stellenbosch
7599

Tel: (021) 881 3881
Fax: (021) 881 3000

RUSTENBERG ESTATE

No eye-catching wine route sign, just an unobtrusive pointer takes wine lovers along a winding grass-verged road. Round a final bend the vista opens to display a Cape jewel: the Schoongezicht homestead, set against a mountain backdrop, with vineyards climbing the slopes. Beside it, enclosed by the traditional *werf* wall, a 200-year-old wine cellar.

Rustenberg's wine making history dates back to 1692, and since 1892 wine has been bottled at the cellar for an unbroken period. This estate prides itself on its historical background, which allows it to claim that a truly European-style wine is produced here.

The introduction of a second label, Brampton, was to augment the estate's premium Rustenberg wine. Named after the bloodline of the farm's champion Jersey herd, the Brampton range is mouth-filling and easily accessible. There are two dry, fruit-packed whites: a fresh, floral Sauvignon Blanc and an unoaked Chardonnay. The Brampton red varies from a Cabernet to a Cabernet-Merlot blend, depending on vintage. The range of slopes and aspects at Rustenberg allows site-specific plantings that enhance the characteristics of its cultivars.

The vineyards, expanded from 65 ha (160 acres) to 125 ha (309 acres), have been upgraded and rejuvenated with a mix of virus-free clones on different root stocks. Wine under the Rustenberg label is made from selected vineyard blocks, vinified separately to maximise the estate's unique terroir, then blended for balance, depth and complexity.

Custodian of the rich heritage embodied in the Rustenberg name, owner Simon Barlow emphasises the importance of the estate's link to the past, "for it helps to know where your roots are when planning for the future". And Rustenberg is building for the 21st century. Without disturbing the tranquillity of the *werf*, the old dairy is being expanded and converted into a state-of-the-art wine cellar with improved tasting facilities.

BEVERAGES INCLUDE:
Brampton Sauvignon Blanc, Chardonnay, Cabernet Merlot, Cabernet Sauvignon, and Rustenberg Sauvignon Blanc.

Opening times:
Weekdays: 09:30 – 16:30
Saturdays: 09:00 – 12:30

Rustenberg Estate
P.O. Box 33
Stellenbosch
7599

Tel: (021) 887 3153
Fax: (021) 887 8466

Saxenburg dates back to 1693 when Governor Simon van der Stel granted the land to a free burgher, Joachim Sax. In 1705 the farm became the property of Olaff and Albertus Berg, who gave it its present name.

Saxenburg had a succession of owners, including Lord Charles Somerset and the De Villiers family, until it was acquired by Swiss business-man Adrian Buhrer in 1989. Together with his wife Birgit and their young family, he revived the proud family tradition of Saxenburg's historic past, ensuring the estate's future growth and development.

Situated on the hills above Kuilsriver between the two oceans, the vineyards enjoy ideal soil and climatic conditions and cool breezes from False Bay during the summer months. The winemaker and vineyard staff work closely with nature and share a sense of achievement when producing only the finest.

Nico van der Merwe, Saxenburg's winemaker, was declared South African Champion Winemaker of 1991, and his expertise and dedication assures the continued quality of Saxenburg wines. Nico feels that there must be real harmony between the grapes and the wine, and his control of the vineyard and wine cellar, combined with the sharing of his knowledge and skills with his staff, enables Saxenburg to produce wine of exceptional quality.

With a spectacular view from the terrace and the tranquillity of the countryside, the Guinea Fowl Restaurant is ideally situated for business lunches, dinners or that special occasion, and is also available for wedding receptions and other private functions. The combination of a menu created to complement Saxenburg wines and a caring, professional staff makes the Guinea Fowl a very special place to visit.

BEVERAGES INCLUDE:
The Guinea Fowl range of white and red wines; a Private Collection of choice reds; the Les Deux Mers range, which includes the unique Grand Vin Blanc and Rouge; select wines of the Château Capion in the Languedoc area of southern France; and Méthode Cap Classique sparkling wine.

Opening times:
Weekdays: 09:00 – 17:00
Saturdays: 09:00 – 16:00
Sundays: 10:00 – 16:00 (November to February)

Saxenburg Wine Farm
P.O. Box 171
Kuilsriver
7580

Tel: (021) 903 6113
Fax: (021) 903 3129

SIMONSIG

Simonsig is situated in South Africa's premium wine growing region. The estate dates back to 1692, and more than 300 years of wine making history at the Cape of Good Hope manifests itself in some of the world's finest wines.

In 1953 Frans Malan started wine farming on De Hoop, which became the nucleus of the Simonsig Wine Estate. In 1968 he bottled some of his wines for the first time and sold them under the Simonsig Estate label. The first Riesling and Chenin Blanc were carefully bottled by hand and personally labelled in his home by his wife Liza.

From these humble beginnings originated a new challenge which grew into a dedicated family business with a proud heritage. Two years later, in 1970, Frans bottled the first red wine which soon became the benchmark for Pinotage in the years to follow.

But Simonsig is best known for its Kaapse Vonkel which was the first South African sparkling wine made using the Cap Classique method – the 1992 Kaapse Vonkel received the wine magazine's Sparkling Wine of the Year award in London.

In 1983 Frans Malan's sons, Pieter (marketing director), Francois (farmer) and Johan (winemaker and cellar master) formed a unique partnership to manage the fast growing business. The current production exceeds 180 000 cases of which more than 40 per cent is exported to more than 20 countries.

BEVERAGES INCLUDE:

White wines like Chenin Blanc, Sauvignon Blanc, Weisser Riesling, Adelblanc, Vin Fumé, Mustique, Chardonnay, Sonstein, Gewürztraminer and Franciskaner. Red wines like Tiara, Shiraz, Frans Malan Reserve, Adelberg, and Pinotage. Cap Classique, sparkling wines, dessert wine, and port.

Opening times:
Weekdays: 08:30 – 17:00
Saturdays: 08:30 – 16:30
• Cellar tours at 10:00, 15:00 on weekdays, and Saturdays at 10:00.

Simonsig
P.O. Box 6
Koelenhof
7605

Tel: (021) 882 2044
Fax: (021) 882 2545

SPIER

An enchanting cultural experience awaits you at Spier, the 300-year-old wine farm near Stellenbosch, home of South Africa's oldest dated wine cellar. Surrounded by rolling vineyards and dramatic mountain vistas, Spier's historic Cape Dutch buildings and beautiful riverside gardens set the stage of a permanent celebration of the finer things in life: delicious food, superb wine, fine art and music.

At the Spier Wine Centre you can taste and compare the best of South Africa's wines under one roof – it is a complete wine route in itself, offering an extensive range of Cape and international wines, as well as their own product. Spier's wine experts will also assist you in creating a unique cellar of your own.

Spier has a restaurant to match every mood. Café Spier offers light lunches, cake and coffee. Hearty pub lunches and merriment galore are the fare of the Taphuis Grill and Riverside Pub. For the best treat in the winelands, there's the Jonkershuis where you can savour authentic Cape dishes in true gourmet style.

Live music is an integral part of the life and soul of Spier and classical music and jazz can be enjoyed in the restaurants and gardens, while international stars perform regularly in the spectacular open-air amphitheatre.

Spier's farmstall offers the ultimate winelands picnic, an *al fresco* spread served under the oaks on the banks of the sparkling Eersterivier.

The Spier manor house contains important collections of old masters, rare antiques and porcelain, while Die Opstal gives an idea of life on an 18th century Stellenbosch wine farm. Die Opstal can also be hired for banquets, weddings and board meetings.

Spier's Cheetah Park is not only a thrilling experience, but by meeting the hand-reared felines you will contribute to the worthy cause of the Cheetah Conservation Fund.

Ponies and old Cape carts can be hired from the Equestrian Centre for leisurely rides through the vineyards.

BEVERAGES INCLUDE:
Sauvignon Blanc, Symphony (a blend of Chenin Blanc and Sauvignon Blanc), Noble Late Harvest, Cabernet Sauvignon, Chardonnay, and a Cabernet Sauvignon and Merlot blend.

Opening times:
• The estate is open seven days a week at the Wine Centre from 09:00 – 17:00.

Spier Management (Pty) Ltd.
P.O. Box 1078
Stellenbosch
7599

Tel: (021) 881 3321
Fax: (021) 881 3634/3087

Stellenbosch Vineyards Ltd was formed in 1996 when four well-known wineries in the Stellenbosch region, namely Helderberg, Bottelary, Eersterivier and Welmoed, merged. The company has 150 growers supplying around 32 000 tons of grapes, which equates to 20 000 litres of wine.

BEVERAGES INCLUDE:
Welmoed, Eersterivier, Helderberg, Genesis and Kumkani ranges, Versus, and Infiniti Sparkling.

Opening times:
Weekdays: 09:00 – 17:30
Saturdays: 09:00 – 17:00 (Eersterivier and Bottelary to 15:00)
Sundays: 10:00 – 16:00 (Welmoed)

Restaurants:
Helderberg Restaurant: open Mondays to Saturdays (bookings: 842 2012)
Duck Pond Restaurant (Welmoed): open Mondays to Sundays (bookings: 881 3310)

Stellenbosch Vineyards Ltd
P.O. Box 465
Stellenbosch 7599

Tel: (021) 881 3870
Fax: (021) 881 3102
E-mail: info@stellvine.co.za

Hans-Joachim Schreiber, owner of Neethlingshof, acquired this farm, then known as Alphen, in 1981. Renamed Stellenzicht Vineyards, it today boasts a reputation as one of the top five farms in the Cape Wine Industry. Stellenzicht's 228 ha (563 acres) of vineyards lie on the slopes of the Helderberg, in the wine-growing area known as the Golden Triangle. The estate was awarded five double gold and four gold medals at the prestigious 1996 Veritas Awards. But 1996 was also a good year internationally – the 1994 Stellenzicht Syrah won the Lyse Cloutier Coffin award, given out for the first time in 1996, as the top wine of the show at Selectiones Mondiales in Montreal, Canada.

BEVERAGES INCLUDE:
Sauvignon Blanc, Heerenblanc, Pinot Gris, Auxerrois, Chardonnay, Gewürztraminer, Weisser Riesling, Fragrance, Stein, Semillon Noble Late Harvest, Weisser Riesling Noble Late Harvest, Muscadel, Cabernet Sauvignon, Merlot, Merlot/Cabernet Franc, Malbec, and Syrah.

For wine tastings and sales please refer to the information under Neethlingshof Estate (page 59).

THELEMA MOUNTAIN VINEYARDS

In July 1983, the McLean Family Trust acquired Thelema, the charming old fruit farm situated on the top of the Helshoogte Pass.

This purchase was the culmination of a long search by Gyles and Barbara Webb for that rare location where exceptional wines could be made.

The farm comprises 157 ha (388 acres) of land on the slopes of the Simonsberg. Elevation ranges from 370 to 640 m (1 214 to 2 100 ft) above sea-level, making Thelema one of the highest, and probably coolest, wine farms in the Stellenbosch area.

There were no vines on the farm at the time of purchase, but the classic varieties that were planted now occupy 37 ha (91 acres), of which two thirds are white varieties.

In October 1987 building started on the winery, and in February 1988 the first load of chardonnay was received and processed. Thelema's policy in the past has been to use only their grapes – wines are bottled on the premises.

Gyles Webb directs all farming and winery operations. His aim as winemaker is to produce flavourful, long lasting dry white and red wines with a distinctive South African character. He is convinced that good fruit is the single most important quality determinant in wine making, so emphasis is placed on vineyard management.

For three years Thelema won the award for the best vineyards in the Stellenbosch region. Some of the accolades received for their wines include the South African Airways trophy for best white wine at the annual SAA selection tasting in 1994, 1995 and 1996 for Chardonnay, and the SAA Trophy for the best red wine in 1995 and 1996 for Merlot and Cabernet Sauvignon. Gyles himself has twice won the Diners' Club Winemaker of the Year award.

BEVERAGES INCLUDE:
Muscat de Frontignan, Chardonnay, Rhine Riesling, and Cabernet.

Opening times:
Weekdays: 09:00 – 17:00
Saturdays: 09:00 – 13:00

Thelema Mountain Vineyards
P.O. Box 2234
Stellenbosch
7601

Tel: (021) 885 1924
Fax: (021) 885 1800

Situated on the slopes of Simonsberg near Stellenbosch, Uitkyk certainly has one of the most beautiful settings in the Cape. The Estate, founded in 1712, is steeped in tradition, yet its wine making facilities are of the most modern available, allowing the estate to keep abreast of the latest viti– and vinicultural practices.

The 600 ha (1 482-acre) estate has about 180 ha (445 acres) under vineyards. A 300 m (984 ft) difference between the highest and lowest vineyards, and a 250 mm (10 in) difference in rainfall means that there are at least a dozen meso-climates on Uitkyk. There are slopes facing in every wind direction and a variety of soils, creating ideal conditions for a variety of grapes. Winemaker Theo Brink produces a Riesling, Chardonnay, Sauvignon Blanc, a Cabernet Sauvignon called Charlonet, and a Cabernet Sauvignon-Shiraz blend. Awards include several Veritas golds, and their 1995 Sauvignon Blanc was the Champion Dry White Wine at the International Wine Competition in Slovenia in 1996.

The magnificent Georgian-style manor house is in complete contrast to the thatch-roofed Cape Dutch architecture on the surrounding farms. Everything about the house, which was completed in 1788, is elegant and the imposing front door was carved by master sculptor, Anton Anreith. Another exciting factor are the impressive neo-classical murals which have been discovered under 13 layers of paint on the original plaster in the hallway. Uncovering and restoring them will take approximately three years. So far, a scene of birds feeding their young in a nest, a nude over the doorway, and a still life of summer fruit have been discovered. Conjecture is, that the murals form part of a whole composition based on the four seasons, but that will have to wait for further discovery.

BEVERAGES INCLUDE:
The Uitkyk range of Riesling, Sauvignon Blanc, Chardonnay, Cabernet/Shiraz, Carlonet, and Shiraz.

Opening times:
Weekdays: 09:00 – 17:00
Saturdays: 09:00 –12:30

Uitkyk Wine Estate
P.O. Box 3
Elsenburg
7607

Tel: (021) 884 4416
Fax: (021) 884 4717

VRIESENHOF

A partnership with nature is the only way to describe the interaction between soil and vine and the wine making skills of Jan 'Boland' Coetzee. His skills were honed during many years as winemaker and consultant to several of the Cape's finest cellars, a season spent as understudy to the winemakers of the prestigious house of Joseph Drouhin in Burgundy, and regular visits to the wine-producing regions of both the new and old worlds.

Jan 'Boland' Coetzee produces his diverse range of wines on two farms, Vriesenhof and Talana Hill which, although they lie next to each other, are worlds apart in soil structure, sun aspects and mesoclimates.

Cradled by the Stellenbosch and Helderberg mountains and facing south towards nearby False Bay, Vriesenhof has a history dating back to the early 18th century. After acquiring the farm, Jan renovated the cellar and pressed his first vintage in 1981. Later years saw the addition of a modern fermentation cellar which blends into the traditionally styled buildings, along with the underground wood maturation cellar.

Adjoining Vriesenhof is Talana Hill, a smaller farm of 7,2 ha (18 acres), which lies in the heart of the Paradyskloof Valley. The vineyards here face southwest towards the familiar outline of Table Mountain in the distance.

Vriesenhof has committed itself to international nature conservation by establishing the Lesser Kestrel Fund. Consequently, 500 numbered magnums are produced annually (this will continue till the year 2 000), the profits of which are donated to the Southern African Nature Foundation. Each vintage release of this special edition features a commissioned work of art by various well known artists.

BEVERAGES INCLUDE:
Vriesenhof Kallista, Vriesenhof Cabernet Sauvignon, Vriesenhof Chardonnay, Paradyskloof White, Paradyskloof Red, Paradyskloof Pinotage, Talana Hill Royale, and Talana Hill Chardonnay.

• Tastings and sales by appointment.

The Wines of Jan 'Boland' Coetzee
P.O. Box 155
Stellenbosch
7600

Tel: (021) 880 0284
Fax: (021) 880 1503

WARWICK ESTATE

Warwick Estate was originally part of the 18th century farm De Goede Success. The founder of Warwick Farm, one Colonel Alexander Gordon, renamed his portion of 'Good Success' in honour of the Warwickshire regiment he had commanded during the Anglo-Boer War.

Stan Ratcliffe bought Warwick in 1964 without a vine on the farm, but possessed the foresight to begin planting the precious cabernet sauvignon vines, which are still used in their wine production today.

With Norma's arrival in 1971, the Ratcliffes made a few experimental wines from cabernet sauvignon, with encouraging results. Their love of Bordeaux wines influenced the planting of two other classic French varieties, merlot and cabernet franc. Warwick's first vintage in 1984 positioned the estate at the forefront of fine wine production in South Africa.

The philosophy which prevails here today is the crafting of handmade wines, meticulous selection of clones, a controlled quality crop and minimal interference in the natural production process. No artificial fining agents or filtration is necessary.

Over the last 10 years Warwick Estate has achieved many successes, international press coverage and much praise from wine lovers all over the world.

The 'Warwick Lady' appears on all of the Warwick wine labels. The gold image comes from the quaint drinking vessel that has pride of place on the Ratcliffe's dining table. This marriage or wager cup was originally used for toasting marriage vows or sealing a wager. When the figure is inverted, both cups can be filled with wine, but the utmost care must be taken when drinking from the larger vessel, so as not to spill the contents of the smaller one and not to put the cup down until all the wine is finished.

BEVERAGES INCLUDE:
Trilogy, Cabernet Sauvignon, Merlot, Pinotage, Tentklip, and Chardonnay.

Opening times:
Weekdays: 08:30 – 16:30
Saturdays: By appointment only.

Warwick Estate
P.O. Box 2
Muldersvlei
7606

Tel: (021) 884 4410/884 4020
Fax: (021) 884 4025

ZEVENWACHT

Sprawling over the Bottelary hills between Stellenbosch and Kuilsriver, Zevenwacht Estate has strong viticultural roots penetrating deep into South Africa's past.

Now comprising some 430 ha (1062 acres), the property was originally two separate farms, Langverwacht and Zevenfontein.

The vineyards, which cover 200 ha (494 acres) are ideally situated for the growing of quality grapes, but perhaps the greatest asset is the cool micro-climate. Varying in altitude from 150 to 350 m (492 to 1 148 ft) above sea level, the vineyards are cooled by the southerly summer breezes from False Bay, only some 15 km (9 miles) away.

The cellar, partly underground, was built during 1982 and here Hilko Hege-wisch is winemaker and cellar master.

In the heart of the vineyards lies the Country Inn with its luxuriously appointed suites. There are also seven vineyard cottages and a chalet, set high on the hills of the estate.

In season, the Pride Restaurant in the manor house is open for breakfast, lunch and dinner throughout the week. Picnic baskets are also available and very popular – guests may relax on the lawns surrounding the lake. There is also a playground for children.

A fully operational banqueting department can organise a variety of functions, from conferences to product launches and weddings. The spectacular venues on the estate offer panoramic views of Cape Town and the winelands. Conference facilities include a high-tech auditorium with sophisticated equipment and professional staff in attendance.

The cheese factory on the farm makes quality cheeses such as matured farmhouse cheddar, mozzarella, provo-letta and feta. These are available for purchase from the wine tasting centre.

BEVERAGES INCLUDE:
Sauvignon Blanc, Pinot Noir/Chardonnay, Blanc de Blanc, Chardonnay, Chenin Blanc, Chenin Blanc/Chardonnay, Rhine Riesling, Bouquet Blanc, Cabernet Sauvignon, Merlot, Pinotage, Shiraz, and Zevenrood.

Opening times:
• Daily from 08:00 – 17:00 at the tasting centre.
• Cellar and vineyard tours by appointment only.

Zevenwacht Wine Estate
P.O. Box 387
Kuils River
7580

Tel: (021) 903 5123
Fax: (021) 903 3373

The town of Paarl (pearl) takes its name from Paarl Mountain which is the second-largest granite outcrop in the world. It lies some 654 m (2 146 ft) above sea level and is famous for three enormous rocks (Paarl, Gordon and Bretagne), whose age is estimated to be around 500 million years.

The Taal Monument (language monument), situated on the slopes of Paarl Mountain, offers panoramic views that stretch all the way to Table Mountain.

Paarl itself is the headquarters for a number of large agricultural, manufacturing and financial companies, houses some of the oldest schools in the Cape, and is home to the Boland Cricket Park.

Paarl is considered a treasure chest of South African architecture. A stroll down Main Street takes the visitor back in time, past superb examples of Cape Dutch, Georgian and Victorian buildings.

Paarl Museum, with its collection of Cape antiques and contemporary exhibitions, is worth a visit. Similarly, the Afrikaans Language Museum in town, which retraces the history of Afrikaans, should not be missed.

For nature lovers there are wildlife centres, hiking trails and cycling routes, and the Paarl Bird Sanctuary is a must for birdwatchers.

Whether it be classical concerts and poetry readings, air flips over the valley, hot-air balloon rides, or a round on the world-renowned golf course, Paarl has something for everyone.

For those who are less adventurous, the town offers a wide range of charming accommodation where the visitor can relax and while away the time with superb wines and gourmet meals.

In order to stay abreast of international standards and to lead the field with regard to quality, the wine estates, co-operatives and small farmers of the Paarl region formed a new organisation called **Paarl Vintners**. Paarl is the first individual wine growing region to formulate a holistic approach, which will address the wine production as well as social issues such as labour conditions.

Paarl Tourism Bureau
216 Main Street
P.O. Box 47
Paarl
7622

Tel: (021) 872 3829/4842
Fax: (021) 872 9376
e-mail: paarl@cis.co.za

Paarl Vintners
P.O. Box 46
Paarl
7622

Tel: (021) 872 3605
Fax: (021) 872 3841
Internet:
http://www.paarlwine.co.za

BACKSBERG

The growth and development of Backsberg is quite remarkable in the South African wine industry, in that it never was a traditional wine farm. Purchased by Mr Charles Back in 1916, the farm was extensively developed by his son Sydney. By the 1960s the vineyards were completely replanted to consist mainly of noble cultivars.

Backsberg vineyards cover a total area of 180 ha (445 acres). The main focus is on the optimum natural ripening of the berries to enhance fruit flavours in the wines. Particular attention is paid to a balanced crop load, with shoot growth and the installation of drip irrigation as a compensatory measure against vine stress.

Modern machinery is used in conjunction with traditional wine making practices to create the quality wines with which Backsberg is associated. Much emphasis is placed on the gentle handling of the grapes to retain the fruit character of the different varietals. All the red wines are aged in French oak barrels for a period of 12–18 months.

Another unique feature of Backsberg is the production of an estate brandy. Sydney Back set about finding the best methods to produce an equivalent to the fine cognacs of France, yet with its own distinctive character. He was rewarded when his first release was awarded the Domecq Trophy at the International Wine and Spirit competition in London for 'best brandy in the world'.

Backsberg Estate believes that the making of fine wines is a holistic process, encompassing all stages from the growing of the young vine to the bottling of the finished product. Furthermore, wines should be priced to reach the tables of as many wine drinkers as possible so that all can share in the magic that is Backsberg.

BEVERAGES INCLUDE:
Chardonnay, John Martin (wood-matured Sauvignon Blanc), Klein Babylonstoren (Cabernet Sauvignon and Merlot blend), Pinotage.

Opening times:
Weekdays: 08:00 – 17:30
Saturdays and non-religious public holidays: 08:00 – 13:00

Backsberg Estate
P.O. Box 1
Klapmuts
7625

Tel: (021) 875 5141
Fax: (021) 875 5144

BERG & BROOK

Visit the Berg & Brook Cellar, and you'll be welcomed by not only one or two, but five identical gables.

Established in 1906, this historic cellar was built on a farm originally granted to Huguenot Minister Pierre Simond in 1688. It played a major role in the formative years of the South African wine industry – yet today, its many gables tell a brand new story.

When two idealistic wine experts come together, great things are bound to happen. Such was the case when well-known wine writer and marketer, Graham Knox, and multiple award-winning winemaker, Nico Vermeulen, took over and rejuvenated the cellar in 1993. They renamed it Berg & Brook and, in combining their knowledge and skills, formulated an innovative philosophy: hand-crafted wines from hand-selected vineyards.

The Berg & Brook Cellar lies on the northern slopes of the Simonsberg mountains, where a picturesque brook meanders through the countryside. This is prime wine-growing land, and most of its grower-members are situated within a 10 km (6.2-mile) radius of the cellar. Resembling the exclusive vineyards of Burgundy, each member has an average of only 7,5 ha (18.5 acres) under vines.

What really distinguishes the Berg & Brook Cellar however, is the fact that they source their grapes not only from surrounding vineyards. The cellar has also commissioned a number of selected growers all over the Western Cape to identify and nurture precious qualities in their vineyards. This has resulted in a range of wines offering not only consistent quality, but also an exciting blend of complex flavours within each wine.

It is Nico Vermeulen's belief that the winemaker should respect the qualities of each selected yield. It is this approach that has led to the variety of styles and generosity of flavours for which the Berg & Brook range is becoming famous.

BEVERAGES INCLUDE:
The Berg & Brook range of Brookside Blanc, Sauvignon Blanc, (unwooded) Chardonnay, Bouquet Blanc, Special Late Harvest, Brookside Red, Merlot, Ruby Cabernet and Cabernet Shiraz, the Savanha range of Chardonnay (barrel-fermented), Sauvignon Blanc, Cabernet Sauvignon, Pinotage and Merlot.

Opening times:
Weekdays: 08:30 – 17:00
Saturdays: 08:30 – 12:30 from September to May.

Berg & Brook
P.O. Box 19
Simondium
7670

Tel: (021) 874 1659
Fax: (021) 874 1402

BOLAND WINE CELLAR

Boland Wine Cellar pressed its first grapes, some 3 000 tons, in 1948. Built on a section of the farm Nieuwedrift on the outskirts of Noorder-Paarl, the co-operative wine cellar served an initial 18 members.

Today Boland Cellar has over 110 members supplying an annual 20 000 tons of grapes from a wide area surrounding the Paarl Valley, including Durbanville, Klipheuwel and Paardeberg.

The farsightedness of the production team and farmer-members in starting a cultivar guideline plan and innovative quality-grading system – implemented vigorously and precisely – has, during the past three years, resulted in an almost peerless rise in the quality of its products. The result is unbeatable value for money.

In 1995, Boland Wine Cellar's wines received two double gold Veritas Awards, one gold, and no less than ten silver awards. The 1992 Cabernet Sauvignon was selected by the esteemed panel of the Wine-of-the-Month Club as the best-value-for-money of its kind, while the 1995 Riesling was awarded similar honours by both the Oaks Wine Club and the Wine-of-the-Month Club.

In order to offer visitors something really special – besides the exceptional wines – Boland Wine Cellar has a charming tasting venue. The fact that it's situated underground contributes to its unique atmosphere. During the festive season visitors can enjoy light meals here, and in the winter months a special programme is offered, with convivial get-togethers centring particularly around Boland Wine Cellar's winter wines. The cellar also specialises in private wine tastings for wine clubs.

BEVERAGES INCLUDE:
A variety of red and white wines, as well as !Um Hap (Sauvignon Blanc and Chenin Blanc blend), !Um Hap Red (Cabernet Sauvignon and Merlot blend), port, white muscadel, sparkling wine.

Opening times:
Weekdays: 08:00 – 17:00
Saturdays: 08:30 – 12:00
Saturdays: 08:30 – 15:00 in season
(December – January)

Restaurant:
Weekdays: 11:00 – 15:00 in season.

*Boland Wine Cellar
P.O. Box 7007
Noorder-Paarl
7623*

*Tel: (021) 862 6190
Fax: (021) 862 5379*

DE ZOETE INVAL

The land on which De Zoete Inval lies was originally granted to one Hercule des Pres (Hercules of the Meadows) by Simon van der Stel 1688.

Robert Frater arrived here in 1878 to find the original cellar, which now houses the tasting room, and vineyards in production on the farm.

Since then the estate has been a paragon of the Boland's traditional family estate and the Frater family has been making wine here for more than 115 years. Today, Adrian Frater and his eldest son, Gerard, the fifth generation on the estate, continue to produce fine wines of singular character, an art developed over three centuries.

For many years port was made for KWV, the highlight of which was the General Smuts trophy awarded for the Grand Champion Wine at the South African Wine Show in 1955. Since then the demand for port has declined, cabernet sauvignon cultivars were planted on a big scale and dry red wines have been produced. More recently chenin blanc, sauvignon blanc and chardonnay have been planted and some interesting white wines are made.

De Zoete Inval applies organic farming methods its 62 ha (153 acres) planted to vines. The grapes are picked ripe, even if the sugars get a little too high, to create individualistic wines in the traditional European style.

The tasting centre has become a popular meeting place for family, friends and visitors. It is managed exclusively by the family, who are always happy to broaden your knowledge, and refine your experience of and feeling for wine.

BEVERAGES INCLUDE:
Late Harvest, Blanc de Blanc (five and two years old), Capri, Blush, Rosé Sec, Yvette (dry, fruity white). Grand Rouge, Chloë (dry, wooded red), Cabernet Sauvignon, Réserve, and extra dry red.

Opening times:
Mondays to Saturdays: 09:00 – 17:00

De Zoete Inval
P.O. Box 591
Suider-Paarl
7624

Tel: (021) 863 2375
Fax: (021) 863 2817

Peacocks scatter as you turn off Suid-Agter-Paarl Road and drive up to Fairview. Past the famous goat tower, which delights adults and children alike, a warm welcome awaits in the tasting room, where a large selection of wines and cheeses are to be sampled.

When Charles Back's grandfather bought the farm in 1938, wine making was already established – folklore tells of a doctor who prescribed teaspoons of the farm's wine to ill children.

Charles Back was recognised as South African Winemaker of the Year in 1996. Several of the estate's wines have also won acclaim at prestigious events.

BEVERAGES INCLUDE:
Sauvignon Blanc/Chenin Blanc, Weisser Riesling, Pinot Gris, Pinot Gris/Riesling, Crouchen/Chardonnay, Chenin Blanc, Semillon, Gamay Noir, Pinotage, Shiraz, Cabernet Sauvignon, Bouquet Fair.

Opening times:
Weekdays: 08:00 – 17:00
Saturdays: 08:30 – 13:00

Fairview
P.O. Box 583
Suider-Paarl
7624

Tel: (021) 863 2450
Fax: (021) 863 2591

Historic Fredericksburg is situated on the northern slopes of the Simonsberg, midway between the beautiful towns of Paarl and Franschhoek.

The farm was founded by brothers Jean and Daniel Nortier over three centuries ago, and covers 90 ha (222 acres).

In the 1980s, the vineyards were replanted with noble grape varieties.

RdeR, Rupert de Rothschild Vignerons, is a partnership between Anthony Rupert Jnr and Benjamin de Rothschild, the son of Baron Edmond de Rothschild. The Rothschilds are the owners of Bordeaux Crû Bourgeois Chateau Clarke in Listrac, France, and partners in Chateau Lafite-Rothschild.

BEVERAGES INCLUDE:
RdeR wines are Chardonnay and Sauvignon Blanc, Standard Fredericksburg are Sauvignon Blanc, Chardonnay and Cabernet Sauvignon.

• Fredericksburg will be open to the public after completion of its new cellar early in 1998.

Fredericksburg
P.O. Box 55
Simondium
7670

Tel: (021) 874 1648
Fax: (021) 874 1802

GLEN CARLOU

Nestled high in the foothills of the Simonsberg Mountains, looking northward towards Paarl, lies Glen Carlou Vineyards which was established by the celebrated winemaker, Walter Finlayson, in 1985. This farm has already developed a firm reputation among connoisseurs for its exquisite wines, both here and abroad.

The 108 ha (267-acre) farm once formed part of the original Simonsvlei land grant Skilpadjie, named after the now endangered geometric tortoise, and was given the name Glen Carlou by a previous owner in honour of his three daughters, Lena, Carol and Louise.

Walter Finlayson, perhaps one of South Africa's best known winemakers, has devoted his life to the production of fine wines. In recognition of his success, he has twice been awarded the coveted Diners' Club Winemaker of the Year Award. Over the past 20 years, his wines have received medals and trophies too numerous to mention and have regularly been Wine of the Month of the South African Airways.

Walter's son, David, has now joined the company as cellar master, having gained experience overseas after vintages in Australia and Bordeaux (France). He was trained at Elsenburg College in South Africa.

Since January 1996, Glen Carlou has been associated with one of the most prestigious cellars in California, the Hess Collection Winery.

Only cultivars best suited to the climate and soil type, like cabernet sauvignon, pinot noir, merlot, cabernet franc, petit verdot and chardonnay, have been planted in the 39 ha (96 acres) of vineyards.

BEVERAGES INCLUDE:
Chardonnay, Devereux, Pinot Noir, Les Trois, Grand Classique, Merlot and Port.

Opening times:
Weekdays: 08:30 – 16:45
Saturdays: 09:00 – 12:30

Glen Carlou
P.O. Box 23
Klapmuts
7625

Tel: (021) 875 5528/5396
Fax: (021) 875 5314
e-mail: glencarlou@wine.co.za

KWV

The cellar complex of the KWV (Kooperatiewe Wijnbouwers Vereeniging) Cellars in Paarl covers an area of 22 ha (54 acres) – the largest co-operative cellar in the world.

KWV Brandy Cellar in Worcester is the largest of its kind in the world, with 120 copper pot stills under one roof. (Due to evaporation, 14–16 bottles of brandy a year are lost from each barrel. This is known as the angels' share.)

A team of 12 tour guides presents tours in English, Afrikaans, German, French and Scandinavian languages. Educational tours for school groups, technical tours for wine specialists, and tours in other languages can be arranged by prior reservation.

The cellar tour visits the Maturation House Cellar where the famous red wines mature to perfection, the hand-carved vats in the renowned Cathedral Cellar, as well as the five largest vats in the world. The tour is concluded with an informal tasting of a range of award-winning wines and brandies which are available in 53 countries.

KWV is capable of handling large groups and informal wine tastings for up to 250 visitors on reservation, and are also happy to arrange incentive tours (i.e. by steam train). During the December holidays, walk-in tourists can enjoy a video show and wine tasting, separate from the cellar tour.

Paarl is a town of many cultures.

Among the most awe-inspiring experiences is the sound of the Khuthele School choir singing Xhosa songs in the KWV Cathedral Cellar, or watching 'gumboot' dancers performing in the cellar.

Wines produced by the KWV are mainly destined for the export market.

Opening times:
Weekdays: 08:00 – 16:30
Saturdays and public holidays: 08:30 – 16:00
Sundays (48 hour reservation only): 10:00 – 14:30

• Scheduled tours take place Mondays to Saturdays and public holidays.
Afrikaans: 09:30
German: 10:15
English: 11:00 and 14:15
French: 15:00 on Wednesdays only.
Scandinavian languages: must be booked 48 hours in advance.

KWV
P.O. Box 528
Suider-Paarl
7624

Tel: (021) 807 3007/8
Tel/Fax: (021) 863 1942

LABORIE CELLAR

Laborie wine estate and its beautifully restored manor house, declared a national monument, are the possession of KWV International.

The renaissance of the magnificent Laborie wine estate in Paarl was completed with the opening of its new tasting facility, underground barrel maturation cellar and sparkling wine fermentation cellar on 27 November 1996. Their completion brought the estate in line with the most modern wineries in South Africa and added another pearl to Paarl's collection.

The barrel maturation cellar has a capacity of 860 (300-litre, 528-pint) barrels, and the sparkling wine fermentation cellar can contain three vintages of Cap Classique (21 000 litres, 36 960 pints per vintage) and two vintages of Blanc de Noir sparkling wine (60 000 litres, 105 600 pints per vintage).

Laborie's wines have proved their worth in abundance. At the International Wine Challenge in England, the 1995 Chardonnay and 1995 Pinotage won silver medals. Most exciting of all, the 1992 Cap Classique received a double gold Veritas Award and the 1995 Pinotage a gold medal (this wine was also chosen as South African Airways Wine of the Month in August 1997).

The excellent techniques applied by the superb teams of the vineyard and the cellar, are reflected in the demand for this vineyard's quality products and the estate's future is bright.

The convivial new tasting room has a panoramic view over the vineyards, valley and Drakenstein mountains. It is one of the most scenic tasting venues in the Cape winelands and offers daily tastings, enabling visitors to sample the estate's newest selection of wines in elegant surroundings. The public is informed about the estate and its interesting history.

BEVERAGES INCLUDE:
Traditional Cap Classique, Blanc de Noir, Sauvignon Blanc, Chardonnay, a red blend of Merlot/Cabernet (Bin R88), Pinotage, Pineau de Laborie, Merlot, Cabernet Sauvignon and the Estate Brandy.

Opening times:
Weekdays: 09:00 – 16:30
Saturdays: 09:00 – 12:30
• Cellar tours by appointment only.

Laborie Cellar
P.O. Box 528
Suider-Paarl
7624

Tel: (021) 807 3390
Fax: (021) 863 1955

Landskroon's wine making tradition dates back to the arrival of French Huguenot settlers in the late 17th century. Among the newcomers was Jacques de Villiers, a winemaker from Niort in France. In 1874 his great-grandson Paul bought a portion of the original Landskroon farm which had been granted to a free burgher by Governor Simon van der Stel in 1692.

Expansion followed until, today, Landskroon comprises over 600 ha (1 483 acres) – with vineyards covering nearly 300 ha (741 acres).

Landskroon is still in the de Villiers family, currently being managed by Paul and Hugo de Villiers. Paul's son, Paul jr, represents the ninth generation carrying on the proud family tradition in wine making.

Although Landskroon is primarily known for its port and red wines, the estate also produces an excellent range of white wines. Landskroon's port won numerous awards over the years, among them inclusion on South African Airways First Class winelist, champion status at both the Paarl Wine Show and South African Wine Show, and a gold medal at the Veritas Awards.

For the hungry day visitor the estate offers a vintner's platter served under stately oaks, from where there is a delightful view over the farm and Table Mountain. For those wishing to stay longer, a self-catering, elegantly furnished chalet, serviced daily, offers an opportunity to relax and unwind in beautiful surroundings.

Landskroon wines can also be labelled with your private labels (minimum order of 10 cases of any one type of wine) – contact the office for further details.

BEVERAGES INCLUDE:
Chenin Blanc Dry and Semi-Sweet, Sauvignon Blanc, Pinot Gris, Pinot Blanc/Chenin Blanc, Bouquet Blanc, Blanc de Noir, Cinsaut/Shiraz, Cinsaut, Pinotage, Shiraz, Merlot, Cabernet Sauvignon, Cabernet Franc, Red Port, White Morio Muscat Jerepigo and natural grape juice.

Opening times:
Weekdays: 08:30 – 17:00
Saturdays: 08:30 – 12:30
• Closed on Sundays. Open on public holidays, excluding Good Friday, Christmas Day and New Year's Day.
• Cheeses available for sale.
• Lunches served November – April, weekdays from 11:30 – 14:30.
• For groups, booking is essential.

Landskroon
P.O. Box 519
Suider-Paarl
7624

Tel: (021) 863 1039
Fax: (021) 863 2810

Nederburg, now over 200 years old, traces its origins to 1791, when the deputy Commissioner-General at the Cape granted a tract of land to a German immigrant named Philip Wolvaart who planted the first vines.

Nederburg changed hands several times but it was not until 1937 that a new tradition at Nederburg, and indeed in South African wine making, was founded when Johann Graue became the first South African to use the cold fermentation process.

Nederburg continues to build on the philosophy that quality begins in the vineyard. This is the only commercial wine producer in South Africa that operates an ongoing scientific plant material improvement programme. With a choice of vineyards on farms in various wine-growing areas, Nederburg's viticulturists and winemakers can select the most suitable grapes for the creation of wines sure to satisfy every consumer.

Nederburg has, for years, actively realised its social responsibilities in the community, while cultivation and production practices are environmentally friendly, and conform to international guidelines.

Annual Nederburg opera and ballet merit prizes are awarded to the best artists in the nine provinces, and the annual Nederburg Auction serves as a valuable showcase for South African winemakers and their products.

A visit to Nederburg allows the tourist to share in its proud history and taste award-winning wines. The elegant centrepiece of the farm is the historic Nederburg homestead, a classic example of Cape Dutch architecture.

Cellar tours, including a short audio-visual presentation and a tasting of five of Nederburg's well-known wines, can be arranged by appointment. Light lunches, served under the oak trees, are available by appointment only.

BEVERAGES INCLUDE:
A vast and renowned range of dry, off-dry and semi-sweet white wines, Blanc de Noir and Rosé, as well as red wines, sparkling wines (like the ever-popular Kapsekt), and sweet wines.

Opening times:
Weekdays: 08:30 – 17:00
Saturdays: 09:00 – 13:00
• Closed on Sundays.

Nederburg
Private Bag X3006
Paarl
7620

Tel: (021) 862 3104
Fax: (021) 862 4887

NELSON WINE ESTATE

Arising in the foothills of the Paarl Mountain, Nelson's Creek meanders amid massive trees across the 142 ha (351 acres) of the Nelson Wine Estate.

Nestling among tall trees, the estate is set in a majestic old-world setting where historic buildings have been lovingly restored by the Nelson family to house a beautiful yet modern cellar and conference centre. Old bush vines have been extensively replanted over the past 10 years and the estate is now planted with virus-free clones of the big six: cabernet sauvignon, merlot, pinotage, shiraz, chardonnay and sauvignon blanc.

The wines are truly exquisite, the unique micro-climate of multi-directional slopes and diverse soil types facilitate the production of both white and red wines of exceptional quality.

The estate boasts an array of awards, including the South African champion status for its wooded Chardonnay at the South African Young Wines Show, as well as gold medals for its Cabernet Sauvignon and Reserve Champion South African dry white wines.

• If the Nelsons are at home they will be happy to receive you on Saturday afternoons and Sundays.
• Cellar tours can be arranged on request.

BEVERAGES INCLUDE:
Tinel, Chardonnay, Marguerite, Muscat D'Alexandrie, Albenet, Merlot and Cabernet Sauvignon.

Opening times:
Weekdays: 08:00 – 17:00
Saturdays: 09:00 – 13:00

Nelson Wine Estate
P.O. Box 2009
Windmeul
7630

Tel: (021) 863 8453
Fax: (021) 863 8424

RHEBOKSKLOOF ESTATE

Rhebokskloof Estate dates back to 1692 when Simon Van der Stel gave a free grant to Dirk Van Schalkwyk, and is named after the small buck, rhebok, which used to roam freely in the area and may still occasionally be seen in the vineyards.

The estate nestles in two valleys, adjoined by the Paarl Nature Reserve at the northern end of Paarl Mountain, and is renowned for producing some of the finest wines in the area. Several of its wines have been awarded gold medals at the annual Veritas Awards.

During 1997, the Rhebokskloof Merlot 1995 was judged to be the 9th-best Merlot in the world at the World Wine Festival in Switzerland.

The estate boasts the award-winning Victorian and Cape Dutch restaurants, which are not named for their cuisine, but after the architectural style of the buildings in which they are housed. In the colder months, patrons are able to enjoy the gourmet delights in cosy dining rooms, while in summer the scrumptious meals, prepared by executive chef Stefan Achterfeld, are served on a terrace overlooking the beautiful gardens, vineyards and mountains.

Visitors are invited to enjoy top-quality wines produced by winemaker, Danie Truter, in the special tasting room.

BEVERAGES INCLUDE:
Chardonnay Sur Lie, Chardonnay Grande Reserve, Grand Vin Blanc, Charsau,

Requiem (Weisser Riesling), Weisser Riesling, Gamay Noir, Cabernet Sauvignon, Dry Red, Bouquet Blanc, Harvest White, sparkling wine.
The estate also produces a fine Extra Virgin Olive Oil.

Opening times:
Mondays to Sundays: 09:00 – 17:00 including public holidays.
• The restaurants are open every day of the week (except Wednesdays). Open if Wednesday is a public holiday.

Rhebokskloof Estate
P.O. Box 7141
Noorder-Paarl
7623

Wine sales:
Tel: (021) 863 8386
Fax: (021) 863 8504

Restaurant:
Tel: (021) 863 8606
Fax: (021) 863 8906

RUITERSVLEI ESTATE & SIMONSVLEI WINERY

Ruitersvlei's micro-climate makes it one of South Africa's prime wine-growing regions. It is run by father, John Faure, and his daughters, Nicolette, Belinda, Theresa and Sheryl.

Traditional wine making methods and scientific research enable the Faure family to determine the best location for noble cultivars, in order to create exceptional wines. Grape varieties are specially selected for their compatibility with the varying soils and micro-climates at the different altitudes.

Ruitersvlei offers beautiful views and the curio shop contains handmade crafts.

BEVERAGES INCLUDE:
Chenin Blanc, Chenin Blanc Chardonnay, Paarl Riesling, Mountain Side Red, and White, Special Late Harvest, Cabernet Sauvignon, Pinotage, Merlot, Cinsaut, Cinsaut Cabernet Sauvignon.

Opening times:
Weekdays: 08:30 – 17:30
Saturdays: 08:30 – 13:00
• Closed on religious holidays.

Ruitersvlei Estate
P.O. Box 532
Suider-Paarl
7624

Tel: (021) 863 1517
Fax: (021) 863 1443

In the shadow of the impressive Taal (language) Monument, wines of exceptional quality are produced by Simonsvlei, one of South Africa's leading wine producers and exporters.

The winery was established in 1945 on the initiative of Sonny le Roux, who served as first chairman. Determined to provide the area's farmers with the facilities and expertise to produce high-quality wines, his vision has since been fulfilled – excellent wines at affordable prices have become the hallmark of Simonsvlei Winery.

This is the only cellar to have received the President's Award for export achievement twice in a row, in 1994 and 1995.

BEVERAGES INCLUDE:
The Simonsvlei and Mount Marble ranges.

Opening times:
Weekdays: 08:00 – 17:00
Saturdays: 08:30 – 16:30

Simonsvlei Winery
P.O. Box 584
Suider-Paarl
7624

Tel: (021) 863 3040
Fax: (021) 863 1240

Brad's Kitchen
Tel: (021) 863 2486

VEENWOUDEN

Situated on the northern side of Paarl with spectacular views over the Klein Drakenstein Mountains, lies Veenwouden, a small boutique winery belonging to international opera singer, Deon van der Walt.

Living in Europe, and having travelled extensively, gave Deon the opportunity to sample some of the greatest vintages available. This persuaded him to buy the 18 ha (44.5 acre) table grape farm Ebenaezer in 1988, and change it into the wine farm Veenwouden.

The first van der Walt to land at the Cape in 1727 hailed from Veenwouden, a tiny hamlet in Friesland, in the Netherlands. Deon's parents, Charles and Sheila, agreed to settle on the farm to manage it in his absence.

Since Veenwouden is a very small winery it was decided to plant only the noble cultivars and to limit the yield to a maximum of 5 tons per hectare to attain wine of the best possible quality. Initially, consultant winemaker Giorgio Dalla Cia from Meerlust was assisted in the Veenwouden cellar by a young French winemaker. Towards the end of 1993 Marcel, Deon's brother, joined the team, handling the 1995 harvest after working and studying at Chateau Le Bon Pasteur in Pomerol, Bordeaux (France) under the guidance of world renowned oenologist Michel Rolland.

The little boutique cellar was designed to combine elements of both the old-world as well as the new-world wine areas. Dark cypresses flank its ochre-coloured walls, while the tasting area is beautifully decorated with handpainted frescoes.

Since the launching of Veenwouden's wines in August 1995 they have received accolades from all over the world. In December 1995 Veenwouden's Merlot was selected to be served in the Metropolitan Opera House.

BEVERAGES INCLUDE:
Veenwouden Vivat Bacchus, Veenwouden Merlot and Veenwouden Classic.

• Tastings by appointment only.

Veenwouden Private Cellar
P.O. Box 7086
Noorder-Paarl
7623

Tel: (021) 872 6806
Fax: (021) 872 1384

Villiera Estate

The wine making tradition of the Grier family began in the 1970s with cousins Jeff and Simon qualifying as oenologist and viticulturist respectively. Their pursuit of wine making excellence found a home in 1983 with the purchase of the Villiera Estate in the Paarl Region.

Extensive replanting of classic varietals, and updated cellar facilities for both still wine and Méthode Cap Classique production were implemented, laying firm foundations for the outstanding wines produced by this dedicated family team.

The white wines extend from the classic varietals of Sauvignon Blanc, Blanc fumé (wood fermented), Chardonnay, Chenin Blanc, Gewürztraminer and Rhine Riesling to the blended Blue Ridge Blanc and Sonnet. These fine white wines reflect the variety of style, soil types and climatic conditions which characterise the Villiera Estate.

The reds all benefit from careful oak maturation to achieve maximum flavour enhancement. The wines range from the early maturing Blue Ridge Rouge to Cabernet Sauvignon, Merlot, Pinotage and Crû Monro, which can all be aged for up to 10 years.

In certain vintages Villiera Estate will produce a port to compliment its stable of fine red wines. Villiera tradition established the Grier family name in the world of wine. This pioneering partnership, together with Jean Louis Denois of the Champagne region, France, has resulted in the production of bottle fermented Méthode Cap Classic sparkling wine.

Beverages Include:
Carte Rouge, Brût Rosé, Carte D'Or, Vintage Brût.

Opening times:
Weekdays: 08:30 – 17:00
Saturdays: 08:30 – 13:00
• Open on public holidays.

Villiera Estate
P.O. Box 66
Koelenhof
7605

Tel: (021) 882 2002/3/4
Fax: (021) 882 2314

Windmeul Co-op Wine Cellar was established in 1944 and presses an average of 13 000 tons of grapes which are received from a wide area, stretching from Agter-Paarl, Wellington and Paardeberg to Malmesbury.

More than half the grapes are produced from bush vines which are only irrigated supplementarily. The cultivars used at present are 80 per cent white and 20 per cent red. Within the next 4 years this distribution will change to 60 per cent white and 40 per cent red. All newly established vineyards are of noble cultivars and the micro-climate is carefully chosen to achieve maximum aroma from the different cultivars.

At present new equipment is being installed in the cellar, enabling the winemaker to meet future demands. The emphasis will be on fruitiness and full-ripe tannins. Presently, wines are mainly sold to Stellenbosch Farmers' Winery, though small quantities are available directly from the cellar. Stormy Cape Chenin Blanc, which is sold to restaurants in England, is the only export product of Windmeul Co-op Wine Cellar Limited at present. Hein Koegelenberg is the manager-winemaker and Johan Joubert the assistant winemaker.

BEVERAGES INCLUDE:

Chenin Blanc, Sauvignon Blanc, Cinsaut, Pinotage and a Cabernet Sauvignon and Merlot blend with good ageing potential.

Opening times:
Mondays to Fridays: 08:00 – 17:00
• Tastings by appointment only.

Windmeul Co-op Wine Cellar
P.O. Box 2013
Windmeul
7630

Tel: (021) 863 8043
Fax: (021) 863 8614

ZANDWIJK WINE FARM

In 1689, Willem van Wyk settled on a tract of land nestling on the slopes of Paarl Mountain. As a farmer he was a dismal failure and it was only in 1742, when the farm was sold to Jacobus Bosman, that real development of Zandwijk began.

Bosman bought the farm as a young man, owning only a horse and two male slaves. At the time of his death in 1782 he left his family a well-developed wine farm.

By the time Cape Gate (Pty) Ltd discovered Zandwijk in 1983, it had changed hands 22 times and fallen into disrepair, producing only table grapes and plums. But the farm was ideally situated and an elegant setting for the creation of superior kosher wines. All that was needed was a reputable wine-maker. Nathan Friedman, Executive Director of Cape Gate, offered Leon Mostert the position. Having cleared the grounds, planted the vineyards and built a new wine cellar incorporating the most up-to-date technology, Leon Mostert went to Israel for an intensive course on the making of kosher wines.

Creating a distinctive wine under the restrictive kosher laws is a challenge few winemakers would rise to. All operations must be supervised by the Beth Din and in some cases the winemaker may not deal with the wine on a 'hands-on' basis. The cellar is closed and all operations cease on the Sabbath, and it is essential that only additives from kosher origins are used. Leon's ambition is to produce kosher wines that will far surpass the best kosher wines currently available – wines for those who see tradition as a way of life.

BEVERAGES INCLUDE:
Klein Draken Dry White, Weisser Riesling, Sauvignon Blanc, Chardonnay, Kiddush, Cabernet Sauvignon and grape juice.

Opening times:
Weekdays: 08:00 – 12:30 / 13:30 – 17:00
• No sales or tastings take place on Saturdays, Sundays and Jewish holidays.

Zandwijk Wine Farm
P.O. Box 2674
Paarl
7620

Tel: (021) 863 2368
Fax: (021) 863 1884

ZANDDRIFT VINEYARDS

The small size of Zanddrift allows this vineyard the freedom to try out new techniques. Continual experimentation ensures that cultivars are perfectly matched to the terroir, while an innovative approach in the cellar produces wines of top quality.

Of the total 45 ha (111-acre) area, 29 ha (72 acres) are currently planted under traditional Cape varieties like chenin blanc, semillon, chardonnay and pinotage, which flourish in the sandy loam and decomposed granite soils.

Two large dams, filled each winter by the two rivers running through the farm, provide overhead and micro-jet irrigation of the vineyards.

Extensive soil and canopy management, together with environmentally friendly farming methods, establish the high quality of the grapes long before the harvest is brought in.

Harvesting is done either early in the morning or late in the afternoon, to ensure that the grapes stay as cool as possible, in order to enhance their aroma and natural flavours.

Wines are made in the new-world style by means of controlled cold fermentation, both in the steel tanks and by means of chilling plates in the new French oak casks.

BEVERAGES INCLUDE:

Klein Draken, Weisser Riesling, Sauvignon Blanc, Chardonnay, Kiddush, Nouveau, red and white grape juices.

Opening times:
Mondays to Fridays: 09:00 – 17:00
• Weekends by appointment only.

Zanddrift Vineyards
P.O. Box 541
Paarl South
7624

Tel: (021) 863 2076
Fax: (021) 863 2081

Scenic Wellington, situated at the foot of the Hawekwa Mountains, is often called the Boland's best-kept secret. Many picturesque wine farms, handed down from generation to generation, are tucked away in the foothills of the spectacular mountain range.

The town grew out of an outpost at the limit of early Cape expansion, and played a vital role in the wagon-building industry which explains its early name *Wagenmakers Vallei* (the wagon makers' valley).

Today, Wellington is an important educational centre – the country's oldest teacher training college is situated here, as is the Huguenot College for the training of mission and social workers.

The town's atmosphere is captivating – the people are very hospitable, will welcome you warmly and introduce you to a host of attractions.

There are many historical buildings such as the Dutch Reformed Church, and the old blockhouse on the Hermon road, which was the southernmost fort built by the British forces during the Anglo-Boer War.

Be sure not to miss the Wellington Museum, whose interesting exhibits range from Egyptian antiquities to a collection of historic photographs and documents from the Huguenot Seminary and the College archives.

Granny's House contains a unique and priceless collection from a bygone era, while Grandpa Jasper's clay pigeon shooting range will provide hours of fun and excitement – rifles and ammunition are available and *lapas* (shelters) are provided for *braais* (barbecues) and *potjiekos* (tasty meals prepared in a traditional three-legged cast iron pot).

Then, of course, there is the splendid outdoors. Head for the vine cutting nurseries, where more than 90 per cent of South Africa's vineyard plant material is cultivated, and the Bain's Kloof Pass, which has been declared a national monument. It offers hiking and horse trails, and some of the most exquisite wildflowers to be seen in spring (September).

At De Slangerivier berry farm visitors can pick their own strawberries from as early as the middle of July. The farm also produces berry jams, herb vinegar, mustard and frozen vegetables and is open all week.

A stay in Wellington is an experience of true hospitality. A wide variety of accommodation and conference facilities is available. Contact the Information Office for particulars.

Wellington Tourism Bureau
104 Main Road
P.O. Box 695
Wellington
7654

Tel: (021) 873 4604
Fax: (021) 873 4607

BOVLEI

Bovlei was established in 1907 and is the second oldest co-operative winery in South Africa. For the past 80 years, Bovlei Cellar has been producing the most palatable wines in this area. This can be attributed to the excellent soil from which the wine grape extracts its treasure.

Currently, 73 members supply approximately 10 000 tons of grapes to Bovlei annually. The cellar, which has some of the most modern processing facilities available, obtains its grapes from mainly three areas: Agter-Groenberg, Bovlei and Leeuwrivier. All three areas are blessed with good, warm soil (essential for the preparation of full dry red and sweet wines), and cool soil for quality white wines. Grapes for Bukettraube, Sauvignon Blanc, Weisser Riesling and Riesling are mainly obtained from the cooler slopes of the Bovlei and Leeuwrivier areas, where slightly gravelly and sandy soils predominate. Cabernet sauvignon, pinotage, cinsaut and shiraz grapes are cultivated mainly in the warm soils of the northern slopes of Agter-Groenberg. For the preparation of full-sweet wines, grapes with a higher sugar content are needed and these are obtained from the warm slopes of the Bovlei and Leeuwrivier areas.

BEVERAGES INCLUDE:

Choice white wines like the semi-sweet Blanc Imperial, Bukettraube, Weisser Riesling, Gewürztraminer, Special Late Harvest, Chenin Blanc, Sauvignon Blanc, *Riesling and Chardonnay.*
Red wines feature Grand Rouge, Pinotage, Shiraz, Merlot, Cabernet Sauvignon and Ruby Cabernet, as well as Hanepoot, Muscat d'Alexandrie and port.
There are also sparkling wines and red and white grape juice.

Opening times:
Weekdays: 08:00 – 12:30 / 13:30 – 17:00
Saturdays: 08:30 – 12:30

Bovlei
P.O. Box 82
Wellington
7655

Tel: (021) 873 1567/864 1283
Fax: (021) 864 1483

CAPE WINE CELLARS

The wines of Cape Wine Cellars feature the very best from four of the Paarl Wine of Origin's leading wine cellars. The four cellars – Wamakersvallei, Wellington, Bovlei and Boland – each a producer of fine wines in its own right, have joined forces with the SAD Group to form Cape Wine Cellars, producers of Kleinbosch and Cape Safari wines.

From the grapes grown by 305 farmers in the Paarl wine region, the very best of varietal vintages are selected for the Kleinbosch range. The wines are vinified by the four cellars and finally selected by Cape Wine Cellars' master blender, Jeff Wedgwood.

Noble cultivars like cabernet sauvignon, merlot, chardonnay and pinotage make up the core of the range. Every year an exceptional Chenin Blanc will be selected for inclusion in the Kleinbosch range, bottled fresh and young to capture the crisp tropical fruit flavours and yeasty overtones of new wine.

The Cape Safari range of 'lifestyle wines' include several delectable blends spearheaded by Stardust White, an off-dry, fruity blend of Chenin Blanc, Colombar and Riesling, and Late Sun Red, a soft, smooth dry red made from cinsaut and cabernet sauvignon. More full-bodied blends of Chenin Blanc, Sauvignon Blanc, a Cinsaut-Cabernet Sauvignon and a Pinotage make up the rest of the current range.

Cape Wine Cellars has been active in the export market since 1995, with various different labels being exported to various countries. Kleinbosch is the flagship brand, with labels like Limiet Vallei, Fonteinkloof, Twist Niet, Goede Kap, Vergeet-my-nie and Morning Mist going to specific foreign markets. A 'flying winemaker' has recently joined forces with CWC and, in 1997, produced his first vintage for clients in the UK.

BEVERAGES INCLUDE:
Various ranges for export. The two local ranges are:
KLEINBOSCH – Chenin Blanc, Chardonnay, Merlot, Pinotage, Cabernet Sauvignon.
CAPE SAFARI – Pinotage, Sauvignon Blanc and Chardonnay blend, Late Sun Red, Cinsaut/Cabernet Sauvignon, Chenin Blanc/Chardonnay.

Opening times:
Mondays to Fridays: 08:30 – 13:00 and 14:00 – 17:00
Saturdays: 08:30 – 12:00
• Tastings at the SAD shop at 11 Main Road, Wellington.
• Dried fruit products sold at the shop.

Cape Wine Cellars
11 Main Road
Wellington
7657

Tel: (021) 873 1101
Fax: (021) 873 3112

JACARANDA

A visit to Jacaranda, smallest wine estate in the Cape with its unique Cellaronda, is a must if you are looking for something different. Owner-winemaker Jan Tromp transformed a circular area around his irrigation reservoir into this ingenious little cellar with its cosy tasting room. Visitors are welcomed with a personally guided tour before tasting his interesting selection of Chenin Blancs.

The wine estate that dares to be different – Jacaranda's aim is to produce wines with a difference. Their chenin blanc vines (average age 20 years), together with particular soil and climatic conditions, produce a very distinctive taste and the very first bottling achieved rare recognition in competition with other Chenin Blancs. This wine is already three years old and is continuing to improve in the bottle.

So far, four different wines have been bottled and the 1996 Jerepigo (also Chenin Blanc) shows promise. Three years ago a small number of cabernet and merlot vines were planted. The single barrel of wine wrested from these vines augurs well for the future. The grapes were harvested early to avoid overtaxing the young vines, producing a reasonably light-bodied blend of distinction which should be very drinkable sometime in 1998.

Tasty olives accompany the tastings and are available for sale, together with delicious cottage cheese. These come,

respectively, from one old olive tree and the pet Jersey cow, Boopsy Daisy.

This charming little estate is situated just 3 km (1.8 miles) north of Wellington on the old Hermon road. When visiting it is best to phone ahead, especially when there is snow on the mountains.

BEVERAGES INCLUDE:
Dry whites like Chenin Blanc Schuss and Chenin Blanc, and off-dry white wine like Chenin Blanc Wedel.

Opening times:
Mondays to Saturdays: Visitors are welcome at any time during daylight hours.

Jacaranda
P.O. Box 121
Wellington
7654

Tel/Fax: (021) 864 1235

WAMAKERSVALLEI WINE CELLAR

Known as Val du Charron (valley of the wagon) in earlier days, this cellar lies in the heart of the Boland. The 12 000 tons of grapes pressed here annually come from farms around Wellington, Hermon and Riebeek-West. The vineyards are spread in between the mountains, where cooler conditions protect the best cultivars against the hot summer sun.

Since 1941, Wamakersvallei winery has proved that they can produce excellent wines, chosen and produced with the utmost care and finesse. This results in wines of exceptional quality, crowned annually with prestige awards at Veritas and other national wine shows – achievements obtained under the guidance of manager-winemaker Chris Roux, and winemaker Pieter Rossouw.

Excellent quality always remains a priority at this cellar, where new technical developments are continually implemented to adapt to modern wine making methods. Highly sophisticated apparatus, like a fully mechanised red wine preparation system consisting of specially designed stainless steel tanks and modern pneumatic Bucher bag presses, are used.

This wine cellar produces an interesting range of quality wines. Recently the winery made a worthy tribute to the history of its town by releasing two new wines under the trademark 'The Duke of Wellington'. These two were selected from the cellar's best wines, and are named Victory Red (a fine blend of Pinotage and Ruby Cabernet) and Chardonnay.

BEVERAGES INCLUDE:
Riesling, Sauvignon Blanc, Chardonnay, The Duke Chardonnay, Skin, Late Vintage, Cinsaut, Pinotage, The Duke Victory Red, Cabernet Sauvignon, Hanepoot Jerepigo, port, sparkling wine, red and white grape juice.

Opening times:
Weekdays: 08:00 – 13:00 / 14:00 – 17:00
Saturdays: 08:30 – 12:00

Wamakersvallei Wine Cellar
P.O. Box 509
Wellington
7657

Tel: (021) 873 1582
Fax: (021) 873 1592

One of the first buildings to catch the eye in Wellington is that of the Wine Cellar with its flags, red roses and dazzling white gables.

In 1996, alterations to the existing red wine cellar were necessitated by the increasing demand for the cellar's wines both locally and overseas. A total of 13 temperature-controlled fermentation tanks was installed. The blending of skins and juice for colour extraction became computer controlled. This increased capacity by approximately 12 000 hl (263 964 gallons). Each year, 49 members harvest 11 000 tons of grapes.

The red wines are the result of perfect climate and soil conditions, and are aged in the cellar's own oak vats. Awards include the trophy for South African Champion Red in 1992.

BEVERAGES INCLUDE:
A range of red and white wines, as well as Jerepigo, port and white grape juice.

Opening times:
Weekdays: 08:00 – 17:00

Wellington Wine Cellar
P.O. Box 520
Wellington
7654

Tel: (021) 873 1257
Fax: (021) 873 2423

Picturesque Welvanpas, where wine has been made and exported since 1705, has been home to the Retief family for seven generations.

This is the farm where Voortrekker hero, Piet Retief, grew up. It is steeped in Afrikaans history and the traditions of the Boland. Presently, the farm is managed by the father-and-son team, Dan and Dan Retief junior.

A range of slopes and soils suits most any noble vine's strictest requirements. High rainfall, altitude, and dedicated management contribute to the ability of winemaker, Dan junior, to make some of the Cape's best wines. New plantings will enlarge the range in the near future.

Welvanpas is one of only a few farms with a nursery to produce its own grafted vines, ensuring the highest quality.

BEVERAGES INCLUDE:
Sauvignon Blanc, Bukettraube, Pinotage and a full-bodied Cabernet Sauvignon.

Opening times:
Weekdays: 09:00 – 12:00 / 13:30 – 17:00
Saturdays: 09:00 – 13:00

Welvanpas Wines
P.O. Box 75
Wellington
7654

Tel/Fax: (021) 864 1258

PREVIOUS PAGE Many wine farms lie in the fertile Hex River Valley. In June, when the vineyards glow in vivid autumn colours, the surrounding mountains are often dusted with snow.
(Hein von Hörsten/Struik Image Library)

LEFT Groot Constantia Estate in the lush Constantia Valley was developed by Cape Governor Simon van der Stel in the 17th century.

RIGHT At elegant Constantia Uitsig, the emphasis is on unhurried wine tasting and leisurely dining.

BELOW Steenberg Vineyards in Constantia offers golf enthusiasts a challenging 18-hole championship golf course.

HEIN VON HÖRSTEN/STRUIK IMAGE LIBRARY

LEFT Klein Constantia is one of
the most picturesque wine estates in
the Constantia Valley.
(Erhardt Thiel/Struik Image Library)
ABOVE Buitenverwachting's wine tradition
goes back to 1825, when Ryk Arnoldus Cloete
planted the first vines.
RIGHT At L'Avenir grapes are hand-picked
for ripeness and taste.

COURTESY OF L'AVENIR ESTATE

LEFT The beautiful, landscaped gardens at Spier have become a popular destination for locals and tourists alike.
BELOW Morgenhof's well-kept formal garden is an impressive sight.
RIGHT Neethlingshof Estate lies at the end of a 1 km (0.6-mile) avenue of pine trees.

LEFT At Hartenberg Estate in Stellenbosch, red wines are matured in French or American oak barrels for a period of 18 months.
BELOW Delheim is beautifully situated on the slopes of the Simonsberg.
RIGHT Charming Lanzerac Manor and Winery is a proud 300 years old.
BOTTOM RIGHT The Blaauwklippen range of wines is popular with connoisseurs.

TOP LEFT The goat tower of Fairview
has become a well-known feature in
the Paarl Valley.

LEFT Laborie's stately old
manor house has been declared
a National Monument.

ABOVE The estate of Fairview, near
Paarl, commands a majestic view of
the valley below.

RIGHT Landskroon, in the Paarl
Valley, is especially renowned for
its superb port and red wines.

1 0 7

LEFT The cellar complex of the KWV is the largest co-operative cellar in the world.
BOTTOM LEFT Wine making at the historic Nederburg Estate dates back some 200 years.
RIGHT The charming wine tasting venue of Rhebokskloof in Paarl exudes atmosphere and character.
BELOW McGregor Winery is one of the wine farms on the increasingly popular Robertson Wine Route.

LEFT Dieu Donné is
dwarfed by the majestic
Franschhoek Mountains
towering above it.
BELOW Choice wines are
made from the vineyards
of Bellingham in the
Franschhoek Valley.
RIGHT Boschendal,
in the Franschhoek Valley,
is one of the oldest wine
estates in the country.
(Alain Proust)

DENNIS GORDON

ALAIN PROUST

110

ABOVE The five magnificent old camphor trees on Vergelegen, in the Helderberg region, have been declared National Monuments.

LEFT Some connoisseurs consider the Vintage Reserve Port of Die Krans to be the best in the country.

BELOW In an alp-like setting reminiscent of southern Europe lies Boplaas Estate in the Klein Karoo.

FRANSCHHOEK

No stay in the Cape would be complete without a visit to the village of Franschhoek that nestles in a beautiful valley surrounded by mountains, just 45 minutes from Cape Town.

Visitors to the Valley of the Huguenots will be just as tempted to stay as the first settlers were 300 years ago. The museum in Lambrecht Street, next to the Huguenot Monument, gives an insight into the daily life of the early Huguenot pioneers. It tells the story of a small group of French Huguenots who landed at Saldanha Bay just over 300 years ago. These Protestant refugees, driven out of France by the relentless persecution of their faith, were granted farms in the most distant outposts of the Cape by Governor Simon van der Stel.

Many settled in Franschhoek, then known as Olifantshoek (elephant's corner), because migrating elephants had trampled a well-worn track through the mountains.

The Huguenots, some of whom came from the wine growing regions of France, had courage and determination, were hardworking, educated and eager to create a new life. Although their numbers were small, their knowledge of viniculture, wine and brandy making contributed invaluably to the economy of their adopted country. Today, this noble tradition is carried forward by the modern wine farmers of the picturesque Franschhoek Valley.

Charming accommodation ranges from luxurious small hotels and beautiful bed-and-breakfast establishments to quaint, self-catering vineyard cottages.

Franschhoek certainly lives up to its reputation as gourmet capital of the Cape. The main street is lined with some of South Africa's most acclaimed restaurants with cuisine to suit every taste and pocket. There are also antique shops, art galleries and boutiques.

A novel way to explore Franchhoek is by bicycle. Guy Younghusband organises groups of up to 12 people who pedal down side roads and dusty farm tracks, stopping off at vineyards to quench their thirst. The tour ends with a relaxing picnic lunch. Either book at the Information Centre, or phone **Winelands Cycle Tours** Tel: (021) 876 2416.

If you prefer something more sedentary, **Horse Drawn Tours**, Tel: (021) 876 2445, will take you on a clip-clopping amble through the vineyards. They also offer a picnic lunch.

Breathtaking scenery and friendly people make Franschhoek a must on any wine lover's itinerary.

Franschhoek Publicity Association
Tel: (021) 876 3603

Vignerons de Franschhoek
Tel: (021) 876 3062
Fax: (021) 876 3603

BELLINGHAM

Set amid one of the most beautiful wine-growing areas in South Africa, Bellingham is rooted in history. Originally known as Bellinchamp (pretty fields), the land was granted to Gerrit Janz van Vuuren in 1693.

Some 250 years later Bellingham acquired another pioneer when self-taught winemaker Bernard Podlashuk bought the farm, upgraded the vineyards and planted new cultivars, producing South Africa's first Rosé, Shiraz and Premier Grand Crû.

The 1980s heralded another phase of a vineyard improvement and renewal scheme, and the beginning of a new cellar development and wine centre.

Having established a tradition for quality, innovation and originality, an additional red wine cellar was built in 1997 to accommodate the ever-increasing demand for Bellingham wines. Bellingham's reputation as a producer of top quality wines resulted in international recognition, a fact evident in its rapidly expanding world-wide market penetration.

In the new cellar complex, elegant and award-winning wines are made by the accomplished winemaker, Charles Hopkins. They range from light white wines to more complex, full-bodied red wines.

Tasty, light lunches are served during December and January, under the stately oak trees that grace the lovely Bellingham estate.

BEVERAGES INCLUDE:
Premier Grand Crû, Grand Vin Blanc, Pinotage, Merlot, Sauvenay, Shiraz, Sauvignon Blanc, Cabernet Sauvignon, Chardonnay, Cabernet Franc, Johannisberger, Classic, Natural Gold, Rosé, and Brût.

Opening times:
Weekdays: 09:00 – 16:30
Saturdays: 10:00 – 12:30 (summer)
• Closed on public holidays.

Bellingham
P.O. Box 134
Franschhoek
7690

Tel: (021) 874 1011
Fax: (021) 874 1690

BOSCHENDAL

Boschendal, near Franschhoek, is one of the oldest estates in South Africa, having been established as 'Bossendaal' by Huguenot Jean le Long in 1685.

Today Boschendal forms part of Anglo American Farms and comprises a total of 3 500 ha (8 648.5 acres). Of this, 491 ha (1 213 acres) – extending along the cool, east-facing slopes of the Simonsberg mountains – are under vine.

The Franschhoek Valley has traditionally been a white wine producing area. Recently the success of the Merlot blend, Lanoy, proved that conditions were favourable for red wines as well. Several new vineyards have been planted to cabernet sauvignon, merlot, shiraz and pinot noir. In turn, these new plantings necessitated the construction of new maturation cellars which were completed in time to vinify the 1997 harvest.

The unique feature of this winery is its fermentation tanks. The suspended tanks are self-draining, so an uncluttered working space is created below. This allows for the pommace to be released into the press which may be driven directly underneath the tanks.

Once in the barrel maturation cellar, the wine can be stored in one of four separate compartments, each with its own temperature and humidity control, once again allowing the reds and the whites to mature at their optimum temperatures.

The Boschendal restaurant complex is a showcase for their wines. Wander through the perfectly restored Cape Dutch manor house (declared a national monument) before indulging in an internationally acclaimed buffet lunch, or wend your way through the oaks to Le Café which serves light lunches and teas. During the summer months Le Pique-Nique offers wicker hampers filled with delectable fresh farm fare. The Taphuis offers conducted tastings throughout the year and vineyard tours during summer.

BEVERAGES INCLUDE:
White wines like Chardonnay Reserve, Blanc de Blanc, Riesling, Blanc de Noir, Chenin Blanc, Le Bouquet, Grand Vin Blanc. Red wines are Lanoy, Méthode Classique, Brut, Brut Rosé and Le Grand Pavillon NV.

Opening times:
08:30 – 17:00 seven days a week.
• Vineyard tours November to April, Mondays to Saturdays at 10:30 and 11:30. Booking essential.
• Cellar tours can also be arranged by advanced booking.

Boschendal Estate
P.O. Box Groot Drakenstein
7680

Tel: (021) 870 4211
Fax: (021) 874 1864

CABRIÈRE ESTATE

Cabrière, the beautiful estate that is situated on the banks of the Franschhoek river, was granted to the French Huguenot Pierre Jourdan on 22 December 1694.

Today, the present proprietor, Achim von Arnim, continues the pioneering spirit by specialising in Cap Classique, and, in the tradition of the Champagne, has named his range of *Méthode champenoise* after the original founder, Pierre Jourdan.

Von Arnim's belief is that wine is grown, not made. This philosophy is symbolised on a sundial in the vineyards dedicated to sun, soil, vine and man.

On 22 December 1994, a new Haute Cabrière cellar and restaurant was opened. This coincided with Cabrière being granted its 'estate' status, and also heralded a shift of emphasis – from being the only specialist in *Méthode champenoise* to becoming more involved in the production of Pinot Noir. The Haute Cabrière cellar, therefore, was specially designed to handle pinot noir, the most fragile, delicate and demanding of cultivars. To achieve this criteria the cellar is unique in structure and situation, positioned as it is on the slopes of the Franschhoek Pass overlooking the Haute Cabrière Pinot Noir vineyards. The grapes enter through the roof of the cellar and the process is totally gravity fed.

The Haute Cabrière Cellar Restaurant, where a quality range of wines compliments choice foods, overlooks the scenic Franschhoek Valley and the vineyards. Wine may be ordered by the glass, and the opportunity to order half portions of food allows guests the gastronomic joy of tasting many different combinations.

BEVERAGES INCLUDE:
The Pierre Jourdan and Haute Cabrière range of wines.

Opening times:
Weekdays: 09:00 – 17:00
Saturdays: 10:00 – 13:00
• Tastings on weekdays: 11:00 and 15:00 and on Saturdays at 11:00.
• Tours by appointment only.

Cabrière Estate
P.O. Box 245
Franschhoek
7690

Tel: (021) 876 2630
Fax: (021) 876 3390

CHAMONIX

Chamonix can be seen spread out below the Franschhoek Pass, making it perhaps the most distinctive of all the farms in the Franschhoek Valley.

Chamonix was originally part of La Cotte, one of the first Huguenot farms. In 1990 it was purchased by its current holding company's investor, who saw the potential and developed it further by building an underground cellar and a French restaurant, La Maison de Chamonix, which won the American Express Style Award in its first year.

Wine connoisseur and owner, Chris Hellinger, together with oenologist Peter Arnold, is producing a limited quantity of wines from specially selected vineyards. 40 ha (99 acres) of the 300-ha (741-acre) farm are planted with vines, and management is continuing the replacement of the older stock with noble varieties.

Overlooking the cellar and shaded beneath ancient oaks, the popular restaurant offers the best in traditional French cuisine, providing a fine à la carte menu, garden menu, cake trolley and full buffet for Sunday lunch.

Spring water was discovered on the farm and found to be among the purest in South Africa. It is now bottled as still, sparkling and flavoured water, and sold under the name Eau de Chamonix.

A fruit schnapps distillery has been built and produces German-style schnapps for a selected market (flavours available are apple, pear, plum, nectarine and mixed fruit). Also produced is CRH Bitters, and a sweeter variety of schnapps in cherry, grapefruit, wild fig and raspberry flavours.

Kamasutra, a smooth-tasting and invigorating elixir, is the latest addition to Chamonix's range of products – a brandy base carefully blended with bitters, as well as exotic herbs like Ginseng and Yorombine, to name but a few.

Guest cottages accommodate visitors wishing to stay awhile.

BEVERAGES INCLUDE:
Chardonnay, Cabernet Sauvignon, Chenin Blanc, Sauvignon Blanc, and Pinot Noir.

Opening times:
• Wine tastings in the Blacksmith's Cottage from 09:00 – 16:00.
• Barbecues/cellar tours on request.
• La Maison de Chamonix closed all day Mondays, and Sunday evenings.

Cape Chamonix Farm (Pty) Ltd
P.O. Box 28
Franschhoek 7690

Tel: (021) 876 2494/8
Fax: (021) 876 3237

La Maison de Chamonix
Tel: (021) 876 2393
Fax: (021) 876 3765

DIEU DONNÉ

Dieu Donné literally translates into 'God given' or 'a gift from God', and the spectacular mountain scenery that may be viewed from these lovely, 10-year-old vineyards certainly endorses this translation.

Situated high on the cool south-western slopes of the Franschhoek mountains, the tempered sun ensures that grapes ripen slowly. This, together with the unique Hutton soil strata, found only in this corner of the valley, allows the cellar master to produce full-bodied, well-balanced wines with a distinctive character.

The meticulously maintained vineyards, owned by the Maingard family, have twice in three years been awarded first prize for the KWV's vineyard block competition, while winemaker Stephan du Toit's wines have achieved several national and international awards. Further recognition was gained when Dieu Donné was awarded the trophy for the best Chardonnay at the International Wine Challenge in 1993.

Dieu Donné, which produces an annual 9 000 cases of wine (95 per cent of which is destined for the export market), is only 45 minutes' drive away from Cape Town. The vineyard is looking forward to increasing its range of wines due to the purchase of additional land which has been planted to include pinotage and shiraz.

Visitors are welcome to call at the vineyard, enjoy the superb scenery, taste the wines and discuss the latest vintages with the winemaker.

BEVERAGES INCLUDE:
Sauvignon Blanc, Chardonnay (Wooded), Chardonnay (Unwooded), Chenin Blanc, Cabernet Sauvignon, Merlot, and Rosé.

Opening times:
Weekdays: 09:30 – 12:30 (winter)
09:30 – 16:30 (summer)
Saturdays: 09:30 – 12:30
(December to January)

Dieu Donné Vineyards
P.O. Box 94
Franschhoek
7690

Tel: (021) 876 2493
Fax: (021) 876 2102

HAUTE PROVENCE

The Haute Provence Vineyards, situated in the Franschhoek Valley, derive their name from the French Huguenots who were settled there in the late 17th century. This is one of South Africa's smaller but best known wineries – and, in terms of quality, certainly one of the top producers in the valley.

Due largely to its innovative young winemaker, John Goschen, it has leaped to the fore in recent times, winning 25 local and international awards in the vintage years 1994–1997. These included two gold medals at the South African National Young Wine Show and two gold medals at the Veritas Awards in 1996, a silver medal for its Chardonnay Semillon blend at the International Wine and Spirit Competition (a first for SA in 1993), and another silver medal for its 1996 Angels' Tears at the World Wine Championships in Chicago in 1997.

In March 1997, Haute Provence's champion 1995 Cabernet Sauvignon was judged the best at a London tasting of 114 premium South African red wines held by Britain's *Wine Magazine.*

Despite having won the Wellington Trophy two years in succession for its 1995 and 1996 Cabernet Sauvignon, Haute Provence is mainly a white wine producer, especially noted for its Sauvignon Blanc and Chardonnay, and was the first South African vineyard to produce a Chardonnay-Semillon blend.

The winery is well known for its Angels' Tears, a special sweet-dry blend which has become its best-seller and winner of several awards.

Production in 1997 was 270 000 bottles, 30 per cent of which were exported, mainly to Great Britain and the United States.

The Haute Provence homestead and cellars are pleasantly situated under large oak trees, and visitors leave with a special memory of warm hospitality in its charming tasting room hung with paintings by famous South African artists past and present.

BEVERAGES INCLUDE:
Brût, Angels' Tears, Chenin Blanc, Semillon, Sauvignon Blanc, Chardonnay, Cabernet Sauvignon, and Muscat d'Alexandrie.

Opening times:
Weekdays: 10:00 – 17:00
Saturdays: 09:30 – 13:00

Haute Provence Vineyards
P.O. Box 211
Franschhoek
7690

Tel: (021) 876 3195
Fax: (021) 876 3118

LA MOTTE

In 1695 a piece of land measuring 68 morgen (54 ha or 133 acres), between the Drakenstein Mountain and Olifantshoek, was awarded to Hans Hendrik Hattingh, who hailed from Spier in Germany. He named the farm La Motte after the home town of his French neighbours.

In 1709 the farm came into Huguenot hands when Pierre Joubert bought the farm from Hattingh. His grandson, Pierre, began the first serious viticulture on the farm and built the cellar and lovely manor house in 1752.

Shortly before the turn of the century, La Motte became part of Rhodes fruit farms and in the 1970s the farm was bought by Dr Anton Rupert, who restored the manor house.

With a view to creating a prime wine producing estate, the vineyards were completely replanted with noble grape varieties like cabernet sauvignon, cabernet franc, merlot, shiraz and sauvignon blanc.

Dr. Rupert's daughter, Hanneli, has been in charge of La Motte since 1985. Winemaker Jacques Borman, a graduate from Elsenburg College, is responsible for the wines on La Motte.

Awards won by this estate include several Veritas double golds. The Millennium, a blend of Cabernet Franc and Merlot, won gold at Intervin in North America, was selected by the American magazine *Wine Enthusiast* as national champion, came second in an Australian tasting of 21 international wines, and was awarded a gold medal at Vinexpo in Bordeaux in 1995.

The estate is open to the public for wine tastings and sales in the very impressive tasting room.

BEVERAGES INCLUDE:
Sauvignon Blanc, Blanc Fumé, Cabernet Sauvignon, Shiraz, and a Bordeaux blend called Millennium.

Opening times:
Weekdays: 09:00 – 16:30
Saturdays: 09:00 – 12:00
• Closed on Sundays and religious holidays.
• Groups of eight or more visitors must make an appointment.

La Motte
P.O. Box 94
Paarl
7622

Tel: (021) 876 3119
Fax: (021) 876 3446

LA PROVENCE

La Provence is situated in the middle of the Franschhoek Valley, just 40 minutes from Cape Town. The historic homestead was one of the original wine estates, granted to Pierre Joubert in 1712 by deed of transfer from the then Cape Governor, Simon van der Stel.

La Provence Estate now covers 22 ha (54 acres), of which 14 ha (34.5 acres) are used for the cultivation of grapes. Cultivars of sauvignon blanc, cabernet, chardonnay, chenin blanc, semillon, Weisser Riesling and SA Riesling are all grown on the estate. Additional vines will be planted, for harvesting within the next five years.

In 1984, La Provence became the founder member of 'Vignerons de Franschhoek', an organisation inspired by imaginative fellow wine farmers in the Valley of the Vines. The Franschhoek Valley has subsequently gained recognition as a pivotal point in the Cape Winelands.

For several years guests to the wine farm have enjoyed the historic splendour of the buildings – a national monument and regarded as one of the best-preserved homesteads in the Cape – while tasting the wine in the cellar adjacent to the building.

La Provence is not only a country getaway with an interesting history, but also a tranquil retreat in the heart of the Franschhoek winelands. Modern, luxury accommodation with a unique rustic flavour is offered in the Jonkershuis

cottage, which dates back to 1694 and is believed to have been Pierre Joubert's first dwelling.

BEVERAGES INCLUDE:
Sauvignon Blanc and Chardonnay.

Opening times:
Weekdays: 09:30 – 12:30 / 13:30 – 17:00
Saturdays: 09:30 – 12:30
• Closed on Sundays and public holidays.

La Provence
P.O. Box 393
Franschhoek
7690

Tel: (021) 876 2163
Fax: (021) 876 2616

L'ORMARINS

L'Ormarins is steeped in the old traditions of the French Huguenots. Its first owner was the industrious young Jean Roi who, by 1694, had planted over 4 000 vines on the virgin slopes of the Groot Drakenstein mountains.

As a wine farm L'Ormarins had the early distinction of producing South Africa's first champion brandy and first champion white wine. It was also one of the first South African wine estates to plant sauvignon blanc.

In 1969 a new chapter in the colourful history of L'Ormarins began when the Rupert family bought the estate. In addition to restoring the gracious homestead to its original Huguenot splendour, the estate was completely redeveloped with new and noble varieties.

Under Anthonij Rupert, L'Ormarins is setting new standards in the production of wines of outstanding quality. Grapes are picked at night. The 12 wines produced by the estate have won numerous awards including Veritas double golds, and a gold medal for the 1989 Cabernet Sauvignon at the Challenge International du Vin in Bordeaux in 1996.

Conducted tours take visitors to the modern wine cellar, the original restored wine cellar filled with casks imported from France and carved with the crests of the original Huguenot settlers, and a glorious collection of old copperware. The estate's wines can then be sampled in what must be one of the most impressive wine tasting rooms in the winelands.

BEVERAGES INCLUDE:
Sauvignon Blanc, Blanc Fumé, Chardonnay, Pinot Gris, Rhine Riesling, Guldenpfennig, Grand Vin Blanc, Merlot, Shiraz, Cabernet Sauvignon, Optima, and Port.

Opening times:
Weekdays: 09:00 – 16:30
Saturdays: 09:00 – 12:30
• Tours conducted weekdays at 10:00, 11:30, 15:00 and Saturdays at 11:00.
• Closed on Sundays and religious holidays.

L'Ormarins
Private Bag X 6001
Suider-Paarl
7624

Tel: (021) 874 1026
Fax: (021) 874 1361

MONT ROCHELLE

Mont Rochelle Vineyards belongs to Graham and Lyn de Villiers, 8th-generation descendants of French Huguenot Jaques de Villiers who first planted vines in the Franschhoek Valley over 300 years ago. The farm was named after the French town, La Rochelle, from which the three de Villiers brothers had fled, and was the communal farm granted to them in 1689.

The farm has been completely redeveloped and replanted to noble cultivars. Today sauvignon blanc is grown on the highest east-facing slopes in the valley, cabernet on warm western slopes and chardonnay in a rich alluvial riverbed a few million years old.

Victorian charm and high technology combine to make this state-of-the-art cellar one of the most unique in the winelands. Winemaker Anna-Maree Mostert, a graduate of Elsenburg College with six years' practical experience in The Bergkelder, and vintages in California and France, brings a special kind of caring to the pressing and processing of the grape, producing wines of exceptional quality and flavour.

Visitors are welcome to cellar tours and tastings in the charming old tavern which contains relics of Franschhoek's Huguenot history. Mont Rochelle also has trail rides and horseback cellar tours.

BEVERAGES INCLUDE:
The Mont Rochelle and Petit Rochelle range of wines.

Opening times:
Tuesdays to Saturdays: 11:00 – 16:00
Sundays: 11:00 – 13:00
(September – April)
• Closed on religious holidays.

Mont Rochelle
P.O. Box 334
Franschhoek
7690

Tel: (021) 876 3000
Fax: (021) 876 2362
Cell: 082 447 8941

Equestrian Centre
Tel: (021) 876 2635

MÔRESON SOLEIL DU MATIN

Môreson Soleil du Matin, or morning sun – which now includes the adjoining farm Blois – originally formed part of La Motte, one of Simon van der Stel's original land grants to Hans Hendrik Hattingh in 1695. This beautiful riverside winery nestles in one of South Africa's most picturesque mountain settings in the Franschhoek Valley.

The Friedman family acquired the farm in the mid-1980s and undertook a comprehensive replanting programme of noble varieties, followed by the building of a modern cellar, tasting room and restaurant.

The influential British wine magazine, *Decanter,* awarded the Môreson Chenin Blanc and Cabernet Sauvignon four stars.

Môreson Soleil du Matin has a plush and comfortable wine tasting and sales venue attached to the modern and compact cellar. These buildings are set among the vineyards, fruit orchards and magnificent oak trees. Visitors to Môreson Soleil du Matin can enjoy the fine wines and a Mediterranean farm-style luncheon at the restaurant, Bread & Wine.

BEVERAGES INCLUDE:
Sauvignon Blanc, Premium Chardonnay, Unwooded Chardonnay, Chenin Blanc, Noble Late Harvest and Cap Classique – Soleil du Matin NV, Cabernet Sauvignon, Merlot, Pinotage, and Shiraz.

Opening times:
Tuesdays to Sundays: 11:00 – 17:00
(In season – December to April)
Wednesdays to Sundays: 11:00 – 15:00
(Out of season – May to November)

Môreson Soleil du Matin
P.O. Box 114
Franschhoek
7690

Tel: (021) 876 3112
Fax: (021) 876 2348

Restaurant Tel: (021) 876 3692

PLAISIR DE MERLE

Plaisir de Merle has a rich history dating back to 1678, when the Huguenot Charles Marais and his family left the hamlet of Le Plessis Marly in France and sailed to the Cape of Good Hope to begin a new life.

In 1688, Governor Simon van der Stel settled the Marais family among other Huguenots, on farms in the mountainous splendour of the Berg River Valley, in the Drakenstein area. Charles Marais called his farm Le Plessis Marly, (which gradually changed to Plaisir de Merle) as a tribute to his birthplace. His grandson, Pieter, built up an enviable reputation as one of Groot-Drakenstein's great wine farmers.

Daniel Hugo, having married one of Pieter Marais's daughters, became the next proprietor of Le Plessis Marly. Between 1805 and 1831, under Hugo's auspices, activity was focused on the 60 000 vines and the cellar. The old gabled wine cellar, dated 1831, can still be seen today. The new cellar which houses the wine production was completed in 1993.

Plaisir de Merle was purchased by Stellenbosch Farmers' Winery from its most recent owners, the Gray family, and is today one of the largest wine farms in the Cape, covering 974 ha (2 407 acres).

It has often been said that good wines begin in the soil, and at Plaisir de Merle the quality of the arable land is undeniably excellent. This positive factor, combined with mountain slopes which optimise the exposure of each cultivar to the meso-climatic conditions, and an abundant supply of fresh mountain water, contributes to the excellence of the end product.

Plaisir de Merle's goal has always been the integration of vineyard practice and wine making, thereby producing wines of unsurpassed quality. This philosophy has now borne fruit with the introduction of an exclusive range of wines, designed to find favour with the most discerning palate.

BEVERAGES INCLUDE:
Sauvignon Blanc, Chardonnay, and Cabernet Sauvignon.

Opening times:
Weekdays: 09:00 – 17:00
Saturdays: 10:00 – 13:00

Plaisir de Merle
P.O. Box 121
Simondium
7670

Tel: (021) 874 1071
Fax: (021) 874 1689

RICKETY BRIDGE VINEYARDS

On 13 May 1797 the widow Paulina de Villiers was granted the land that lies nestled against the mountain along the Franschhoek River. The farm, named Paulina's Dal, later became known as Rickety Bridge as a result of the very old and dilapidated bridge (now repaired) that had to be crossed to reach it.

During December 1996, Rickety Bridge Vineyards was taken over by its present owners. Their winemaker, David Lockley, has a passion for the land and the wine, believing that good wine has its origin in the vineyard. The white grapes are picked at nighttime to ensure delivery of cool firm bunches to the cellar.

The old cellar, which was revived during 1995, is gaining acclaim each year. (Lord Rothschild found the wine 'delicious'.) A new cellar is being constructed and will be commissioned for the 1998 harvest. The old cellar will be restored to its former glory and converted into a restaurant (Paulina's) during 1998 as part of the planned Paulina's Drift Retreat and Conference Centre.

Opening times:
Weekdays: 10:00 – 16:30 in season.
• Wine sales, but phone ahead, on Saturdays from 10:00 – 16:30.
• Formal tastings take place at 11:00, 12:30 and 15:00.

BEVERAGES INCLUDE:
Chenin Blanc, Sauvignon Blanc, Semillon and Chardonnay, Merlot and Cabernet Sauvignon. Shiraz and Paulina's Reserve (a blend of Cabernet Sauvignon, Merlot, Cabernet Franc and Malbec), special releases that formed part of the 1997 bi-centennial celebrations, are available only from the estate.

Rickety Bridge Vineyards
P.O. Box 455
Franschhoek
7690

Tel: (021) 876 2129
Fax: (021) 876 3486

VON ORTLOFF

The Von Ortloff name originated in 1686 and the family was raised to the peerage in 1866. Georg and Evi Schlichtmann, current owners of Von Ortloff, have a direct link to this illustrious history. Evi is the granddaughter of Dr. jur. Max Kurt von Ortloff. The Cape Dutch homestead was built in 1820 and the original wine cellar dates back to 1800.

Von Ortloff is dedicated to making wines of unique quality and unsurpassed pleasure. Based on the philosophy that wine making begins in the vineyard, the major replanting program was preceded by a unique process called ridging. This allows for better management of the sandy loam and lime-rich soil with its high proportion of pebbles and clay substructure. The collective result is an ideal micro-climate for growing top-performing cabernet sauvignon, merlot, chardonnay and sauvignon blanc.

Situated on historic Dassenberg farm, Von Ortloff is bordered by mountains and the Franschhoek River. The vineyards lie between 200–300 m (656–984 ft) above sea level, facing north to north-east. The prevalent climate is a precondition for the cultivation of noble cultivars – more temperate than most, the vineyards benefit from an average of 980 mm (38.5 in) of rain per year, while prevailing south-easterly winds cool the grapes considerably, and chilly nights leave a blanket of mist until late morning.

BEVERAGES INCLUDE:
Chardonnay and No. 5 Sauvignon Blanc, Cabernet Sauvignon, Merlot, and No. 7 Merlot.

Opening times:
• Tastings and visits by appointment.

Von Ortloff
Dassenberg Farm
P.O. Box 341
Franschhoek
7690

Tel/Fax: (021) 876 3432
Residence: (021) 876 3710

The towns situated between the Hottentots Holland and Helderberg mountain ranges (Gordon's Bay, Faure, Firgrove, Lwandle, Macassar, Sir Lowry's Pass Village, Somerset West and Strand) are collectively known as the Helderberg.

The area enjoys a mild climate and is conveniently close to Stellenbosch and Cape Town. Many tourists stop here *en route* to the Garden Route.

Among the attractions this region has to offer are: the Helderberg Nature Reserve, which offers several graded walks through an unspoilt natural environment; the harbour of Gordon's Bay with its adjacent sandy beach; the *kramat* (Muslim shrine) in Macassar; and a host of scenic drives, such as the Sir Lowry's Pass and the Helderberg Wine Route.

Visitors can enjoy many watersports, swimming and sunbathing at the lovely beaches along the coast. Golf enthusiasts can choose between four golf courses, one of which, Erinvale, hosted the 1996 World Championships. Hikes and horse riding trails are a must for lovers of the outdoors.

The main town in the Helderberg, Somerset West, holds regular events and festivals. There is a Country Craft Market every Saturday morning from September to May; a 300-stall market right under the sparkling Christmas lights on Main Street at the beginning of December; and an Arts Festival in September which celebrates poetry, drama, cabaret, comedy and music and offers many stalls, exhibitions and a beer tent. For more information get in touch with the Tourism Association.

Accommodation is offered in world-class hotels, guest houses and friendly bed-and-breakfast establishments.

Helderberg Tourism Association
P.O. Box 19
Somerset West
7129

Tel: (021) 851 4022
Fax: (021) 851 1497

128 HELDERBERG

LONGRIDGE WINERY

Longridge, a modern winery in a beautiful, stylish building, is situated on the slopes of the Helderberg Mountains near Somerset West and commands majestic views over the vineyards toward False Bay, with Table Mountain in the distance.

Wine making at Longridge combines the best of modern technology with traditional methods and the uniqueness of its location. Quality is this vineyard's overriding philosophy – wines are nurtured throughout the wine making process and only those deserving of the Longridge name find their way into the bottle and onto the market. Longridge wines consistently achieve acclaim both locally and internationally.

Longridge's experienced winemaker, Danie Zeeman, spends his winters at Domaine Jacques Prieur in Meursault, Burgundy (France), where Martin Prieur is winemaker of one of the most eminent cellars in the world. Martin, in turn, visits the South African vineyard during its harvest, to offer guidance and to expose Longridge to new possibilities that fall outside the mould traditionally set in the Cape.

As part of its holistic approach Longridge imports a number of high-quality wines, notably from Burgundy, the Rhône, Australia, New Zealand, Chile and the USA, all of which are also available for sale from the winery.

The winery has a lovely tasting room where their three highly-rated labels are available for tasting. Picnic baskets and light lunches are available by 24-hour prior arrangement during the holiday season.

BEVERAGES INCLUDE:
Chardonnay, Sauvignon Blanc & Cap Classique Brût, Bayview Chardonnay, Chenin Blanc, Sauvignon Blanc, Bay Blanc & Bouquet Blanc, Capelands Sauvignon Blanc-Chardonnay, Classic Dry White, Sauvignon Blanc-Chenin Blanc, Cabernet Sauvignon, Merlot, Pinotage, Bayview Merlot, Shiraz-Cabernet Sauvignon, and Ridge Red Capelands Cinsaut-Cabernet Sauvignon.

Opening times:
Weekdays: 09:00 – 17:00
Saturdays: 09:00 – 14:00

*Longridge Winery
P.O. Box 1435
Stellenbosch
7599*

*Tel: (021) 855 2004
Fax: (021) 855 4083
Email: longridg@iafrica.com*

Meerlust is one of South Africa's most famous wine estates. The first owner of the farm was Henning Huising, an early German immigrant who became a very wealthy cattle and sheep farmer in the colony. The farm was granted to him by Governor Simon van der Stel in 1693, and he named it *Meerlust* (pleasure of the sea). The Cape Dutch homestead was built by Huising in the 17th century.

In 1757 Johannes Albertus Myburgh bought the estate, and it has been in the Myburgh family for nine generations. The present owner is Hannes Myburgh.

The first estate wine to be produced was the Cabernet Sauvignon 1975, but the wine that put Meerlust on the map was the Meerlust Rubicon 1980.

The first white wine, a Chardonnay, was launched early in 1997. The Estate also produces a new spirit at their distillery: Meerlust Grappa is available from the estate.

Meerlust wines have won a number of awards and gold medals at prestigious American wine competitions, and in 1994 the Meerlust Rubicon 1987 was nominated by the American magazine *Wine Enthusiast* to be one of the world's top 20 red wines.

BEVERAGES INCLUDE:
Cabernet Sauvignon, Rubicon, Merlot, Pinot Noir, Chardonnay, and Grappa.

Opening times:
• The estate is not open to the public but can be visited by appointment.

Meerlust
P.O. Box 15
Faure
7131

Tel: (021) 843 3587
Fax: (021) 843 3513

VERGELEGEN

Vergelegen (meaning 'situated far away') was granted to Willem Adriaan van der Stel on 1 February 1700. The younger van der Stel transformed the uncultivated land into a veritable paradise. He planted vines, camphor trees and oaks, established eighteen cattle stations, dug reservoirs and irrigation canals to control the Lourens River, and built a beautiful homestead. "I saw this estate with exceptional pleasure, since everything there was laid out wonderfully finely" wrote the Reverend Francois Valentijn in November 1705. However, after a bitter dispute with the free burghers, the Dutch East India Company ordered Van der Stel's return to the Netherlands.

Vergelegen passed through a succession of owners, until Anglo American Farms purchased it in 1987. To this day five magnificent camphor trees, which were declared national monuments in 1942, guard the entrance to the homestead. An oak tree planted by Van der Stel also still graces the estate and is thought to be the oldest surviving specimen in South Africa.

Visitors are welcome to stroll through the splendours that are Vergelegen: upon entering the Octagonal Garden, brilliant colours and heady perfumes pay homage to the foresight of Lady Phillips, who from 1917 to 1940 lavished much time and attention on the grounds. The Lady

Phillips Tea Garden is an ideal setting for an alfresco lunch, while the Rose Terrace provides visitors with the opportunity of enjoying refreshments during the summer months. The Heritage Centre incorporates a gift shop and an interpretative centre.

In the making of the wines a simple philosophy is followed: there must be harmony between the old and the new. The lovely design of the winery mirrors the octagonal walled garden laid out by Willem Adriaan van der Stel.

The entrance fee includes a guided tour of the winery and wine tasting.

BEVERAGES INCLUDE:
Cabernet Sauvignon, Merlot, Mill Race Red, Chardonnay, Chardonnay Reserve, Sauvignon Blanc, and Vin de Florence.

Opening times:
09:30 – 16:00 daily in season.
• Winery Tours: 3 tours daily by appointment. No children under 12.
• No tours or tastings on Sundays.

Vergelegen
P.O. Box 17
Somerset West
7129

Tel: (021) 847 1334
Fax: (021) 847 1608

In the early 1800s, a shepherd by the name of Hermanus Pieters followed an elephant path down to the sea, and discovered good grazing land around a freshwater spring, right on the coast.

News of his find spread quickly. Soon entire families arrived, settling down for a few months to graze their livestock and leaving only in winter when grazing was better inland. The plentiful supply of fish attracted fisherfolk and led to a more permanent settlement, named Hermanus Pietersfontein in honour of its discoverer (changed to Hermanus in the 1900s).

The natural beauty, good fishing and healing air of the village were hailed as far away as London, and it became fashionable to journey south in order to convalesce in the 'champagne air'.

Sir William Hoy, one of the first 'tourists' to arrive, strove to maintain the beauty of the village by blocking the extension of the Bot River railway line. To this day Hermanus station has neither tracks not trains.

Hermanus is a haven for outdoor enthusiasts – guided walks, and hikes through the Fernkloof Nature Reserve and the surrounding mountains reveal a diverse display of unspoilt coastal *fynbos*. Bird-watching, fishing, diving, golf and boating are popular, and the soft sandy beaches are a sunworshipper's dream.

The town offers visitors an interesting look into the fishing and whaling history of the area – the old harbour has been declared a national monument. The museum on the slipways exhibits small boats, some over a hundred years old.

Tours at the *perlemoen* (abalone) hatchery near the harbour inform visitors about the life cycle of this endangered shellfish, which is regarded as a delicacy in South Africa and in the East.

However, this town has an even bigger drawing card: the World Wildlife Foundation has recognised Hermanus as one of the best places in the world for whale-watching.

Southern right whales calve in the protected waters of Walker Bay between August and September every year. From rocky cliffs, the whales and their young can be seen as little as 10 m (33 ft) away. Not only that – Hermanus is the only location in the world where a sonar link-up enables watchers to listen to the whales' sounds at the same time. It is also the only place to employ an official 'whale crier', who blows a kelp horn to alert visitors to the whales' whereabouts.

Hermanus Information Bureau
P.O. Box 117
Hermanus
7200

Tel: (0283) 2 2629
Fax: (0283) 70 0305

The Perlemoen Hatchery
Tel: (0283) 2 2140

BEAUMONT WINES

The historic Compagnes Drift in Bot River was once an outpost for the Dutch East India Company in the 1700s, and now functions as a working farm producing a variety of fruits and wine grapes.

When Raoul and Jayne Beaumont started revitalising the old wine cellar in 1993 they made a small quantity of Pinotage from their 5 ha (12 acres) of old vines. The quality of this wine and the subsequent 1994 vintage encouraged them to continue.

Using traditional wine making methods and restored antique machinery, they produced double the amount the following year. The 1995 harvest provided exceptional quality fruit which was picked at optimum ripeness, resulting in an excellent Pinotage which has consistently been rated among the top few in a broad spectrum of wine tastings.

Niels Verburg joined Beaumont Wines as winemaker in December 1995. The 1996 vintage presented a quantum leap for the Beaumonts, with a tenfold increase in their production – from 600 cases to 6 000.

Old tanks were renovated and some new equipment was acquired and it was decided that Beaumont Pinotage and Chenin Blanc, two traditional South African cultivars, would be their flagship wines.

Beaumont is set on the eastern slopes of the Houw Hoek Mountains and falls within the Walker Bay ward, therefore enjoying the influence of a unique, cool maritime microclimate.

Accommodation on the farm is available in the form of comfortable, self-catering cottages.

BEVERAGES INCLUDE:
Pinotage, Chenin Blanc, Sauvignon Blanc, and Chardonnay.

Opening times:
Weekdays: 09:00 – 12:30 / 13:30 – 16:30
• Saturday mornings:
by appointment only.

Beaumont Wines
P.O. Box 3
Bot River
7185

Tel: (02824) 4 9733
Fax: (02824) 4 9733
Cellar: (02824) 4 9450

BOUCHARD FINLAYSON

The vineyards of Bouchard Finlayson are surrounded by a mountain wilderness area rich in fynbos, the unique floral kingdom of the Cape region.

The surrounding mountains form the water catchment area for the vineyards of the Hemel-en-Aarde (heaven and earth) Valley below, where temperatures are kept moderate by the cool breezes from the Atlantic ocean a few kilometres away. The lower slopes of the Hemel-en-Aarde Valley boast heavy, mineral-rich soils which are well suited to the two classic grape varieties of Burgundy: pinot noir and chardonnay.

Peter Finlayson has been making wine in this valley for seventeen years. In 1989 he and Michael Clark acquired the proposed vineyard land. This attracted the interest of Burgundian wine negotiant Paul Bouchard, and the name Bouchard Finlayson was adopted.

For the first wines, grapes were brought in from farms in the Overberg, in the tradition of generations of the Bouchard family. As the production of the vineyard's own grapes increases, however, wine making relies less and less on the role of the negotiant.

Bouchard Finlayson is now planted to 72 000 vines on the Burgundian philosophy of sacrificing yield for greater intensity of fruit. Some 5 ha (12 acres) are planted to pinot noir, and a further 5 ha to the white varietals of chardonnay, sauvignon blanc and pinot blanc.

Wine-making takes place under the dedicated individual attention of Peter Finlayson, and is limited to a maximum of twelve thousand cases. The maturation of Pinot Noir and Chardonnay makes use of oak *barriques* crafted in Burgundy. These barrels are stored in the cool, thatched winery, which looks out through wide verandahs, over the vineyards to the sea.

BEVERAGES INCLUDE:
Pinot Noir, Chardonnay, Sauvignon Blanc, and Blanc de Mer.

Opening times:
Weekdays: 09:00 – 17:00
Saturdays: 10:00 – 12:30

Bouchard Finlayson
P.O. Box 303
Hermanus
7200

Tel: (0283) 2 3515

PAUL CLUVER WINES

Paul Cluver Wines are the result of the vision and creativity of Gunther Brozel, Ronnie Melkh and Ernst le Roux, who, in the mid 1980s, dreamed of exploiting the unique cool climate of the Elgin Valley.

The unique feature of the area is the cool climate which is closer to the climate of Burgundy (France) than that of Stellenbosch. The dream was to make exciting, fruity wines which retained the delicate aromas produced in the cool, slow-ripening vineyards. After much investigation a joint venture was formed with Nederburg and vines were planted. The quality of the first Nederburg wines revealed the potential of the area.

In 1996 the first experimental wines were made on De Rust by the father of the project, Gunther Brozel, who then designed and supervised the construction of a cellar here.

In December 1996 it became a real family venture with Paul and Songvei Cluver's son-in-law, Andries Burger, joining the business as winemaker, and daughter Liesl Cluver as promotional and marketing manager. Both Andries and Liesl had studied viticulture and oenology at the University of Stellenbosch.

The Cluver family believe that their focussed dedication to the quality of the wine has brought an additional dimension to the 1997 hand-crafted Paul Cluver Wines.

There is a tasting room, and pure karakul rugs by artist Volker Berner are for sale, as well as etchings and sculptures by artist Dörte Berner.

BEVERAGES INCLUDE:
Sauvignon Blanc, barrel-fermented Sauvignon Blanc, Chardonnay, Weisser Riesling, Gewürztraminer, Cabernet Sauvignon, and Pinot Noir.

Opening times:
Weekdays: 08:00 – 17:00
Saturdays: 09:00 – 13:00

Paul Cluver Wines
P.O. Box 48
Grabouw
7160

Tel: (021) 859 0605
Fax: (021) 859 0155
Email: liesl@cluver.co.za

HAMILTON RUSSELL VINEYARDS

Located in the cool, maritime Walker Bay appellation, in the beautiful Hemel-en-Aarde Valley behind the old fishing village of Hermanus, Hamilton Russell Vineyards specialises in producing internationally acclaimed Pinot Noir, Chardonnay and Sauvignon Blanc.

Following a prolonged search for the best site to produce South Africa's top cool-climate wines, founder Tim Hamilton Russel purchased 170 ha (420 acres) of undeveloped land in the Hemel-en-Aarde Valley in 1975. The first vines were planted in 1979 and the first wines produced two years later. In 1991 Tim's son, Anthony, took over the management of the Hamilton Russell Vineyards which he has owned since 1994.

Rigorous experimentation with soils, canopy management, clones, root stocks, planting densities, indigenous yeasts, oak and vinification techniques, ensures that the team comes closer and closer each year to realising the full quality potential of the Hamilton Russell Vineyards terroir.

With plantings reduced in 1992 to only the three varieties best suited to the soils and meso-climate, the team, under winemaker Kevin Grant, is able to focus their full energy on creating highly individual wines which express the personality of where they are grown. In the words of Pierre Crisol of French magazine *Gault Millau*, "Drawn from Pinor Noir, Sauvignon Blanc or, as it happens from Chardonnay as in Burgundy, perfectly balanced, they stand without question among the best of the New World".

Low-vigour, stony, clay-rich soils and cool sea breezes from the South Atlantic Ocean less than 3 km (1.8 miles) away, combine with naturally low yields and a long growing season to produce concentrated wines of great individuality and finesse.

BEVERAGES INCLUDE:
Chardonnay, Sauvignon Blanc, and Pinot Noir.

Opening times:
Weekdays: 09:00 – 17:00
Saturdays: 09:00 – 13:00

Hamilton Russell Vineyards
P.O. Box 158
Hermanus
7200

Tel: (0283) 2 3595
Fax: (0283) 2 1797

WILDEKRANS CELLAR

Uniquely situated in the Bot River Valley, just below the Houw Hoek Pass, lies the farm Keerweer on which the Wildekrans Cellar is situated.

Keerweer was purchased by Mr E.K. Green in 1980. Under the guidance of his son-in-law, Bruce Elkin, the extensive planting of cabernet sauvignon, cabernet franc, merlot, pinotage, chardonnay, sauvignon blanc and semillon vines has taken place.

Although wine was made on the farm in the 1930s, the new Wildekrans Cellar, equipped with the most modern wine making facilities, was only completed in 1992.

Wildekrans cellar and its vineyards fall within the Walker Bay ward, whose climate and soil is recognised as potentially excellent for the production of quality grapes. The Atlantic Ocean lies a mere 7 km (4.3 miles) from the farm and plays a very important role in providing the cool sea breezes which temper the macro-climate. The aim is to produce wines with a well-defined personality, reflecting this unique climate, and although the vineyard started producing only in 1993, Wildekrans wines already feature in several award lists.

BEVERAGES INCLUDE:
Sauvignon Blanc, Chardonnay, Pinotage, Chenin Blanc/Sauvignon Blanc, Chenin Blanc Reserve, Cabernet Sauvignon, Cabernet Franc Merlot, and Merlot.

Opening times:
Weekdays: 08:00 – 12:00 / 13:30 – 17:00
Saturdays: 09:30 – 13:00
Sundays: By appointment only.
• Light lunches available by advanced booking.

Wildekrans Cellar
P.O. Box 200
Elgin
7180

Tel: (02824) 4 9829
Fax: (02824) 4 9902

Trade enquiries:
NMK Schulz Fine Wines
Tel: (021) 705 0360
(011) 334 6974
Fax: (0283) 2 2317

WHALEHAVEN

In 1994, when Storm Kreusch-Dau decided to leave the wine making business and spend more time with her daughter, Danica, little did she realise that this was the lull before the storm that was to break a few months later.

A jovial dinner party ended up with Storm committing herself and her family to building a winery, from ground up, in the short time of two and a half months to be ready for the 1995 harvest. And so Whalehaven was born.

The philosophy behind the name is simple and obvious: Walker Bay has become synonymous with the southern right whale. Increasing numbers gather in the bay each year from August to September and it was decided to capture the essence of Hermanus with a name that was distinct and recognisable.

With limited funding and basic equipment, Storm, who holds a BSc degree in oenology and viniculture from Stellenbosch University, set about the project with just a handful of helpers. Land was purchased at the gateway to the Hemel-en-Aarde Valley, and a modern split-level cellar was built to make wines from grapes grown further up in the valley.

The first sod was turned on 5 December 1994 and on 15 February 1995 the first grapes started rolling into the cellar. After a few setbacks, the wines finally settled. On 8 June 1995 the first were released: a Sauvignon Blanc and an unwooded red blend, the 1995 Baleine Noir, both made for early drinking.

Whalehaven produces six wines, two whites and four reds, from grapes bought in from the Overberg wine region.

BEVERAGES INCLUDE:
Unwooded Sauvignon Blanc, Baleine Noire, wood-fermented Chardonnay, Merlot, Cabernet Sauvignon, and Pinot Noir.

Opening times:
Weekdays: 09:30 – 17:00
Saturdays: 10:30 – 13:00

Whalehaven
Private Bag X10
Hermanus
7200

Tel: (0283) 2 1585
Fax: (0283) 2 1917

THE SWARTLAND WINE ROUTE

The Swartland offers the traveller a kaleidoscope of landscapes. Rolling wheat fields abound, interspersed with vineyards which produce high-quality wines. Fruit plantations, protea farms, natural veld flowers and pastures complete the breathtaking picture.

The vineyards of this region, some of which were established in the early 1800s, were linked by the Swartland Wine Route in 1986. This presented a big step forward for the Western Cape tourism industry, especially in view of the fact that the Swartland is a mere 40 minutes' drive from Cape Town.

The route is accessible from all directions and easily links up with the Crayfish Route of the West Coast with its abundant marine life, nature reserves and colourful fishing villages. Excellent roads join the various farms and well-placed sign boards will enable you to reach all of the six cellars with ease.

Towns along the route each offer their own attractions and accommodation. In **Malmesbury**, be sure to visit the beautiful Dutch Reformed Church, built in 1860 and the fifth oldest Dutch Reformed Congregation in South Africa, and the Malmesbury Museum, housed in the old synagogue.

South Africa's biggest oak tree and a privately owned wagon museum are situated on beautiful **Spes Bona** farm on the western slopes of Kasteel Mountain between Malmesbury and **Riebeek West**. Only 3 km (1.8 miles) lie between

Riebeek West and **Riebeek Kasteel**, which have become artists' havens, and offer quaint accommodation, little galleries and coffee shops.

Moorreesburg's Wheat Museum, one of only three in the world with this theme, is well worth a visit. The Dirkie Uys Art Gallery exhibits works of renowned South African painters.

The cannon in **Piketberg** was fired during the 18th century to warn farmers of approaching Hottentots. There are also the old water mill, and Voelvleibos, possibly the largest wild olive forest in the country.

Porterville is a picturesque town on the slopes of the Olifant's River mountains. The old roller mill here has filled sacks of grain for decades and is still in good working order. Visits by appointment, Tel: (02623) 2270.

Swartland Tourism Association
Private Bag X52
Malmesbury, 7300

Tel: (0224) 2 2996
Fax: (0224) 2 2935

Swartland Wine Route
P.O. Box 591
Malmesbury, 7299

Tel/Fax: (0224) 7 1133
swineroute@mbury.new.co.za

Allesverloren is situated on the south eastern slopes of the Kasteelberg, near the little town of Riebeeck West. Dating back to 1704, this historic wine farm produced its first wine in 1806.

The first owners made regular trips to Stellenbosch to attend church and stock up on provisions. This trip by oxwagon took days and, upon reaching home after one such trip, they found that Hottentots had raided their house, burnt it to the ground and stolen all their cattle. Consequently they named their farm *Allesverloren* (all is lost).

In 1872, Daniel Francois Malan bought the farm. It has been in the hands of the Malan family for five generations and was also the birthplace of former premier DF Malan.

The present owner is Fanie Malan and the winemaker is his son, Danie. Awards won by them include the prestigious Trophy de Concours International, won at the world's most important wine and spirits competition, Vinexpo in Bordeaux, in 1989. Their famous port won the L Perold Trophy for Champion Port seven times, the Fawsa Trophy for the best port in its class nine times, and won two Veritas double gold medals.

Recently, the 1991 vintage won gold at The Challenge International Du Vin in France. Allesverloren is the only wine estate in the Swartland Wine of Origin district and is open to the public for wine tastings and sales.

BEVERAGES INCLUDE:
Cabernet Sauvignon, Shiraz, Tinta Barocca, and an award-winning port.

Opening times:
Weekdays: 08:00 – 17:00
Saturdays: 09:00 – 12:00

Allesverloren
P.O. Box 23
Riebeeck West
6800

Tel: (022) 461 2320
Fax: (022) 461 2444

Mamreweg Winery was founded in 1948 and today consists of 30 members who supply it with approximately 10 529 tons of grapes.

Although rainfall in the Darling district is quite poor, vines are not irrigated and farmers have to rely on nature. The limited rains lead to smaller, more concentrated grapes perfectly suited for the making of high quality wines.

Under the watchful eye of cellar master, Daniel Langenhoven, new plantings took place. 1996 was the first year in which wine from noble cultivars was made. To utilise these to their full potential a new red wine cellar was built during 1995, and new wine presses and stainless steel wine tanks were installed to increase capacity.

About 60 per cent of the grapes are white and 40 per cent red. The aim for the near future is a 80/20 ratio between red and white grapes. Late 1997 saw the release, for the first time, of Chardonnay, Cabernet Sauvignon and Sauvignon Blanc under a new label.

Not only are there exciting new wines, but also lovely new labels for the entire Mamreweg range. The theme of these colourful labels is West Coast scenery.

The spectacular wildflower show held in Darling during September is one of the annual highlights of the West Coast region. Mamreweg Winery will release a limited edition of three different 'flower wines' for this show. These will only be available at the Winery and consist of Darling Nemesia (Dry Steen), Darling Kalkoentjie (Chenin Blanc) and Darling Kelkiewyn (Blanc de Noir).

BEVERAGES INCLUDE:
Grand Crû, Dry Stein, Blanc de Blanc, Chenin Blanc, Stein, Late Harvest, Special Late Harvest, Blanc de Noir, Claret, Cinsaut, Tinta Barocca, Pinotage, Cabernet Sauvignon, Cabernet Sauvignon Shiraz, and Hanepoot.

Opening times:
Mondays to Thursdays: 08:00 – 17:00
Fridays: 08:00 – 16:00
Saturdays: 09:00 – 12:00

Mamreweg Winery
P.O. Box 114
Darling
7345

Tel: (02241) 2276/7/8
Fax: (02241) 2647

RIEBEEK WINE CELLAR

Riebeek-Kasteel, the quaint village nestling at the foot of the Kasteelberg about 80 km (50 miles) northwest of Cape Town, is home to the Riebeek Wine Cellar.

Riebeek was the first winery in South Africa to introduce the cold fermentation process back in the 1960s – and it has stayed at the forefront of developments.

Four recently introduced ultra-modern tank presses ensure that large volumes of high-quality wines, especially whites, can be produced. However, the age-old dedication and craft involved in every stage of wine making is lovingly adhered to. Each wine is a product not just of technology, but also of nature and of human care.

A large proportion of the harvest is produced without irrigation, with the resultant low yield and high quality associated with this method.

At the South African National Young Wine Show, the Stellenbosch Young Wine Show and the Veritas Awards, the name Riebeek frequently appears on the winners' list.

In honour of the 17th-century explorer who named the area, Riebeek Wine Cellar launched a very special reserve range under the 'Pieter Cruythoff' label onto the local market.

BEVERAGES INCLUDE:
Chenin Blanc, Colombar, Sauvignon Blanc, Chardonnay, Blanc de Noir, *Weisser Riesling, Late Harvest, Special Late Harvest, Noble Late Harvest, Cabernet Sauvignon, Pinotage, Shiraz, Tinta Barocca, Hanepoot Jerepigo, Red Jerepigo, Port, and Red and White grape juice.*

Opening times:
Weekdays: 08:00 – 12:30 / 13:30 – 17:00
Saturdays: 08:30 – 12:00

Riebeek Wine Cellar
P.O. Box 13
Riebeek Kasteel
7307

Tel: (022) 448 1213
Fax: (022) 448 1281

SWARTLAND WINERY

With the first exploration of the Cape, an area northwest of Cape Town was discovered in 1660 and called *Swartland* (black land), because the indigenous vegetation rhino bush appears to be almost black at certain times of the year.

In 1827, during the period of British control of the Cape, the governor, Sir Lowry Cole, established the town of Malmesbury, naming it after his father-in-law, the Earl of Malmesbury.

In this farming community, renowned for its wheat, sheep and wine farming, 15 farmers met in 1948 and founded their own cellar. Today, just 45 minutes' drive from Cape Town, the Swartland Winery produces and bottles a range of wines from varietals ideally suited to this region.

The farms of the Swartland Winery are scattered within a 22 km (14-mile) radius, covering 3 100 ha (7660 acres) of vineyards in the hills surrounding the town of Malmesbury. In this arid land of warm temperatures and lack of irrigation, bush vines cover 85 per cent of the vineyards, yielding an average of 7 tons of grapes per hectare. Grape selection, therefore, does not occur only by hand but by nature's way. The result is smaller berries with good fruit concentration and ripe, opulent flavour.

The joint vineyard management selects the ideal vineyard position for the cultivar. This, together with the chemical analysis of the grapes in the vineyards, helps the winemaker to produce the quality wines for which Swartland Winery is renowned.

BEVERAGES INCLUDE:
A comprehensive range of dry red and white wines, off-dry, semi-sweet and dessert wines, as well as white and red grape juice and sparkling wine. Select wines are available in 5 l (8-pint) and 2 l (3.5-pint) casks.

Opening times:
Weekdays: 08:30 – 17:00
Saturdays: 09:00 – 12:00
• Cellar tours by appointment only.

Public Relations Officer
Swartland Winery
P.O. Box 95
Malmesbury
7300

Tel: (0224) 2 1134/5/6
Fax: (0224) 2 1750

Winkelshoek is the only private wine producer along this route. The cellar, for many years the property of the Hanekom family, became well known and respected for its unique brandy and range of fortified wines. About four years ago, a West Coast range was launched, which, with its eye-catching labels, became very popular.

BEVERAGES INCLUDE:
Weskus Wines: Blanc de Blanc, Grand Crû, Vin Rouge, Late Harvest, White and Red Jerepigo, Winkelshoek, VO Brandy and Winkelshoek 3 Star Brandy.

Opening times:
Weekdays: 09:00 – 12:00 / 14:00 – 17:00
Saturdays: 09:00 – 12:00

Porterville Wine Cellar was founded on 30 May 1941 by 25 farmers from the Porterville and Piketberg areas. The first grapes were pressed in 1942. Since equal amounts of grapes were received from both regions, it was decided to certify the grapes as coming from the Piketberg area. The cellar today boasts modern facilities able to produce quality wines.

BEVERAGES INCLUDE:
Premier Grand Crû, Sauvignon Blanc, Emerald Riesling, Blanc de Blanc, Chardonnay, Rosé, Late Vintage, Pinotage, Vin Rouge, Golden Jerepigo, Red Jerepigo, White and Red Grape Juice.

Opening times:
Weekdays: 08:00 – 13:00 / 14:00 – 17:00
Saturdays: 08:00 – 11:00

Winkelshoek Wine Cellar
P.O. Box 2
Eendekuil
7335

Tel: (022) 942 1830
Fax: (022) 942 1678

Porterville Wine Cellar
P.O. Box 52
Porterville
6810

Tel: (022) 931 2170
Fax: (022) 931 2171

THE OLIFANTS RIVER VALLEY

The Olifants River valley stretches from Citrusdal in the south to arid Namaqualand in the north, and from the Atlantic Ocean in the west to the boundary formed by the Cape fold mountains – the Cederberg, Gifberg, Matsikamma and Bokkeveld ranges.

This region is renowned for its scenic beauty, its rock formations and, of course, its spectacular show of wildflowers. Every flower season is different, as it is dependent on factors such as the climatic conditions and rainfall. Under normal circumstances, the flowers will bloom from the middle of August to the middle of September. Towns and villages are proud of their natural beauty and show it off to visitors. Good viewing spots are found in the Biedouw and Wuppertal areas, as well as at Garies, Vanrhynsdorp, Kamieskroon, Lambert's Bay and Springbok. An annual flower show is held in Clanwilliam from the end of August to the first week of September.

In the distant past, elephants and other big game roamed the Olifants River region. It was also home to the San Bushmen, and a rich heritage of rock paintings, some of which are believed to be 6 000–7 000 years old, can be seen in places from the Cederberg to the Koebee mountains.

The Cederberg rock formations, such as the Wolfberg Arch, are known throughout the world and hikers, nature lovers and tourists come from far and wide to enjoy the scenic splendours of this rugged mountain region.

The fertile Olifants River valley is intensively cultivated, with emphasis on citrus fruit, vegetables and vineyards. Rooibos tea, a popular healthy drink, is made from a fynbos species endemic to the region.

The seaside villages situated on the West Coast exude a tranquil charm. Of these, Lamberts Bay is undoubtedly the crayfish capital of South Africa. Just off the coast is Bird Island, which is a meeting place for thousands of sea birds.

The Olifants River region presents the visitor with an unequalled diversity of activities and natural beauty.

Olifants River
Tourism Association
P.O. Box 351
Clanwilliam
8135
South Africa

Tel: (027) 482 2024
Fax: (027) 482 2361

Flower Hotline
Cell: 082 990 5395
Tel: (021) 418 3705
Fax: (021) 418 9423

CEDERBERG CELLARS & GOUE VALLEI

Since the first certified wines were made here in 1978, this private cellar has reaped laurels for its excellent, wood-matured red wines. Their distinctive bouquet, colour and delicate balance are attributed to the unique situation of the vineyards: over 1 150 m (3 773 ft) above sea level, and very close to the snow-line.

The wine farm offers the visitor a fine opportunity to combine a visit to the wine route with a peaceful weekend in the mountains: attractive weekend huts on the farm are ideal for this purpose.

BEVERAGES INCLUDE:
Cabernet Sauvignon, Sauvignon Blanc, Chenin Blanc, Bukettraube and Jerepigo.

Opening times:
Weekdays: 08:00 – 12:30 / 13:30 – 18:00
Saturdays: 08:00 – 12:00

*Cederberg Cellars (Pty) Ltd
P.O. Box 8136
Cederberg
8136*

Tel/Fax: (027) 482 2825

In 1660, Jan Danckaert, leader of one of Jan van Riebeeck's scouting parties into the interior, discovered a new valley. After spotting some 300 elephants in the vicinity, he promptly named it the Olifants River Valley.

The original cellar, which made the sweet wines requested by the exiled Napoleon, can still be viewed and the same cultivars are used in Goue Vallei's products today.

The private cellars in this valley had been in existence for over two centuries before they were amalgamated under the Citrusdal Co-operative banner in 1957. Their wines have, since then, been marketed under the Goue Vallei label.

The labels of Goue Vallei's well-known 'flower wine' have become collectors' items since their first release in 1989. Three new members of the Namaqualand or Cederberg flora are depicted every year.

BEVERAGES INCLUDE:
Among others; Chenin Blanc, Blanc de Blanc, Blanc de Noir, Sauvignon Blanc, Rosé, Late/Special Late Harvest, Pinotage, Chianti, Classique Rouge, sparkling wines, still and sparkling grape juice, dessert wines, as well as sherry, port and witblits.

Opening times:
Weekdays: 08:00 – 12:30 / 14:00 – 17:00
Saturdays: 09:00 – 12:30

*Goue Vallei Wines
P.O. Box 41
Citrusdal 7340*

*Tel: (022) 921 2233
Fax: (022) 921 3937*

KLAWER & LUTZVILLE

Klawer, gateway to the Olifants River Valley, offers a warm welcome. Just a stone's throw from the N7, the impressive façade of the Klawer Winery dominates. The attractive building houses the office and sales complex of the cellar, including a tasting room, as well as a large entertainment area. Luncheons for large groups can be arranged by prior booking.

The cellar aims to produce top-quality wines through the limited production of shiraz, sauvignon blanc and merlot.

BEVERAGES INCLUDE:
Mainly white wines (champion Blanc de Noir), sparkling wine and grape juice, Late Harvest, Special Late Harvest, and dessert wines (champion white Muscadel).

Opening times:
Weekdays: 08:00 – 17:00
Saturdays: 09:00 – 12:00

Klawer Winery
P.O. Box 8
Klawer
8145

Tel: (02724) 6 1530
Fax: (02724) 6 1561

Since Lutzville Vineyards was founded in 1962, it has prospered and grown to become the second biggest winery in South Africa.

A unique setting and mild climate – with misty mornings, sunny days and prevailing south-westerly breezes – makes it ideal for growing top-quality grapes. This, together with fertile soil, promotes wines of unique character and outstanding quality.

The wine made from the grapes is marketed under the label Fleermuisklip (the original name of Lutzville was *Vlermuisklip*). The name *Vlermuisklip* is derived from a rock where early travellers, staying overnight, were troubled by bats. On the label is a representation of the bridge (the gateway to Lutzville) where the Sishen–Saldanha railway line crosses the Olifants River Valley.

BEVERAGES INCLUDE:
Red and white wine, sparkling wine, grape juice and Hanepoot.

Opening times:
Weekdays: 08:00 – 12:30 / 14:00 – 17:00
Saturdays: 08:30 – 12:00
• Cellar tours in season must be booked.
• Wine tasting throughout the year.

Lutzville Vineyards
P.O. Box 50
Lutzville
8165

Tel: (02725) 7 1516/7
Fax: (02725) 7 1435

SPRUITDRIFT & TRAWAL WINE CELLAR

Spruitdrift Winery, 5 km (3 miles) outside Vredendal on the R363 route, makes use of technology and equipment that has made it one of the most modern cellars in the winelands.

The cellar experiments with the planting of rare cultivars, which results in interesting blends.

Several awards at wine shows have served to popularise the name Spruitdrift among wine lovers from far and near.

Wine tastings and lectures are regularly conducted in the attractive vinoteque, and snoek (a marine fish) barbecues can be organised for large groups if bookings are made in advance.

Trawal Wine Cellar was established in 1968 and is well known in the area for its quality wines. The cellar is situated next to the N7 route approximately 270 km (168 miles) from Cape Town. The vineyard's location in the cooler part of the Olifants River results in better quality wines, several of which have won awards in regional competitions, as well as the South African Young Wine Show.

This cellar has established a firm name in the export market. Its aim, under the guidance of manager Kobus Basson, and winemaker Alkie van der Merwe, is to produce wine of a high standard and singular character.

BEVERAGES INCLUDE:
Grand Crû, Late Harvest, Special Late Harvest, Hanepoot, Weisser Riesling, Merlot, Pinotage, Cabernet Sauvignon, Chardonnay, Sauvignon Blanc, Riesling, and Red and White Muscadel.

BEVERAGES INCLUDE:
Blanc de Blanc, Late Harvest, Chenin Blanc, Muscat D'Or, Special Late Harvest, Sauvignon Blanc, Chardonnay, Merlot, Pinotage, Travino Spumante (Demi-Sec), Red and White Muscadel, and pure grape juices.

Opening times:
Weekdays: 08:00 – 17:30
Saturdays: 08:30 – 12:00

Opening times:
Weekdays: 08:00 – 12:30 / 14:00 – 17:00
Saturdays: 09:00 – 12:00
• Visitors are welcome to a cellar tour.

Spruitdrift Winery
P.O. Box 129
Vredendal
8160

Tel: (0271) 3 3086
Fax: (0271) 3 2937

Trawal Wine Cellar
P.O. Box 2
Klawer 8145

Tel: (027) 216 1616
Fax: (027) 216 1425

VREDENDAL

The grapes of Vredendal – dale of peace – are grown in soils ranging from river silt to desert grit. They are sugared by the sun and cooled by Atlantic Ocean breezes.

Controlled irrigation coaxes the best from the vines, and such is the size of the winery, that during harvest 160 farmers deliver some 60 000 tons of grapes for pressing. The largest storage tank holds one million litres of wine.

Handling such quantities demands special dedication. Behind Vredendal's success is a three-strong wine-making team, each contributing specific skills, and adamant that the size of the operation has nothing to do with the quality of its product. As one of South Africa's largest wine exporters, Vredendal is committed to quality, both in bulk and boutique wines.

The state-of-the-art cellar is geared to handle smaller quantities, separately and delicately, ageing some of the wines in small oak barrels. It is these wines – fresh and fruity, carefully blended and appealing – that have walked off with major trophies at national wine shows.

BEVERAGES INCLUDE:
Chardonnay, Sauvignon Blanc, Grand Crû, Chenin Blanc, Late Harvest, Stein, Piquant, Special Late Harvest, Spumante, Dry and Semi-Sweet Sparkling Wine, Cabernet, Maskam (a harmonious blend of 3 cultivars), Dry Red, Goiya Kgeisje (a fresh blend of Sauvignon Blanc and Chardonnay), Muscadel Jerepigo, Port, red and white grape juice, Namaqua medium sherry, soet Hanepoot, three- and five-star Namaqua Brandy, and witblits.

Opening times:
Weekdays: 08:00 – 13:00 / 14:00 – 17:00
Saturdays: 08:00 – 12:30

Vredendal Winery
P.O. Box 75
Vredendal
8160

Tel: (0271) 3 1080
Fax: (0271) 3 3476

This picturesque village is famous for its heritage of Cape Dutch and Victorian architecture concentrated mainly in and around Church Street. This, the largest concentration of national monuments in one street, makes the little village unique.

The houses were severely damaged in 1969 when an earthquake, registering 6.4 on the Richter Scale, caused the old structures to crumble. Seismic activity in the area, though not a common occurrence, is associated with a geological fault running in a south-easterly direction just north of Tulbagh.

The natural catastrophe resulted in the masterful restoration of 32 buildings to their original design. This event is celebrated on the last Saturday each October when, with Tulbagh at its most beautiful, Church Street comes alive for the Tulbagh Festival.

The combination of mountains and an extensively cultivated valley make for unparalleled scenery – green orchards and vineyards dominate in the north, and wheat and oat fields characterise the wider, southern section.

The valley is well known for its large variety of colourful veld flowers, many of which are displayed at the annual agricultural show held late in September each year.

Tulbagh offers a variety of museums and sightseeing venues. The Oude Kerk Volksmuseum is the oldest church building in South Africa still existing in its original cross-shaped design. This church, and the three annexes in Church Street, display antique furniture, porcelain and glass collections.

In one of the quaint cottages along Church Street you will find the interesting earthquake exhibition as well as a geological collection. The exhibition gives particulars of several earthquakes that have struck the Western Cape since 1600. It also presents a condensed history of the village of Tulbagh.

The exquisite Vera Humphris collection of miniature houses can be viewed at 4 Witzenberg Street. Vera, who now has 18 exhibits, has been hand-crafting her miniature gems since 1978.

Steinthal, the largest orphanage in the southern hemisphere, lies at the foot of the Witzenberg Mountains, 4 km (2.5 miles) from Tulbagh, and provides a home and sound education for some 560 children. Visits can be arranged. Tel: (0236) 30 1031.

A wide range of accommodation is available, ranging from self-catering bed-and-breakfast establishments to camping places, guest houses and cosy country lodges, situated in and around Tulbagh.

The Tourism Bureau
P.O. Box 277
Tulbagh 6820

Tel/Fax: (0236) 30 1348

DE OUDE DROSTDY & KLOOFZICHT

The graceful manor house of Drostdy, built in 1804, rates as one of the most impressive works of renowned Cape architect Louis Michel Thibault.

Originally the home of the local magistracy, De Oude Drostdy has withstood earthquakes and storms. Since its restoration it serves as museum of cultural history and headquarters of the Drostdy Winery. Established in 1964, it produces wines from choice Western Cape vineyards.

BEVERAGES INCLUDE:
Chardonnay, Merlot, Premier Grand Crû, Claret Select, Stein Select, Late Harvest, Adelpracht, and Drostdy-Hof Extra Light.

Opening times for the wine shop:
Weekdays: 08:30 –12:00 / 13:30 – 17:00
Saturdays: 09:00 – 12:00
Opening times for De Oude Drostdy:
Mondays to Saturdays: 10:00 – 13:00 / 14:00 – 17:00
Sundays: 14:30 – 17:00
Cellar tours:
Weekdays: 11:00 and 15:00
Saturdays: 11:00

De Oude Drostdy
P.O. Box 9
Tulbagh
6820

Tel: (0236) 30 0203
Cellar Tel: (0236) 30 1086

Kloofzicht is one of the very smallest and least significant cellars in the winelands of the Cape. And yet, were it not for that handful of highly individualistic handcrafters, South Africa's wine scene would not only be a little less colourful, but also considerably poorer. Kloofzicht, therefore, is rather important and certainly unique within this context.

Present owner and winemaker, Swiss-born Roger Fehlmann, set foot in the Tulbagh valley for the first time 16 years ago. Here he lived out the home-and-empire-building epoch of his life and immediately began to challenge the belief of local winegrowers, who regard red wines as a categorical no-no.

The farm takes up 16 ha (39.5 acres) of the Tulbagh valley and has cosy and romantic accommodation facilities in store for weary travellers who like to venture off the beaten track.

BEVERAGES INCLUDE:
Alter Ego, Chardonnay, and honey-based mead.

Opening times:
Daily from 10:00 – 16:00

Kloofzicht
P.O. Box 101
Tulbagh
6820

Tel/Fax: (0236) 30 0658

LEMBERG ESTATE

The smaller the estate, the more intimately the vintner can become involved with both the vineyard and the patrons who enjoy its wines.

The 15 ha (37-acre) Lemberg Estate has just 4 ha (10 acres) under vine, allowing German owner and winemaker Klaus Schindler to monitor the vineyards at every stage of development, closely oversee the harvesting and control every facet of the wine making process. Almost all the work is still done by hand, and he also bottles his own wines and designs the labels, ensuring control right up to the final stage. All this leads to wines of exceptional quality with international recognition.

Klaus Schindler produces four distinctive and carefully crafted wines: a Sauvignon Blanc (declared second best among 21 South African Sauvignon Blancs in the year 1995); a fine Hàrslevelü (a tempting rarity in South Africa) made from a grape originating from Hungary where it is blended with other varieties to make the famous Tokaji wine; a full-bodied Pinotage; and, from 1998, a Merlot.

Good wine should round off good food. In the guest house the visitors are treated to delicious, home-cooked meals, home-baked bread, muffins, and scones.

The guest house is a thatch-roofed, spacious and comfortable rondavel with stunning views of the mountains. It has a fully equipped kitchen and its own private garden.

There is a beautiful picnic site at the river and picnic baskets are available by appointment.

BEVERAGES INCLUDE:
Sauvignon Blanc, Hàrslevelü, and Merlot.

Opening times:
Mondays to Saturdays: 11:00 – 12:00 / 13:00 – 15:00
Sundays: By appointment only.
• Light lunches and cellar tours for small groups by appointment only.

Lemberg Estate
P.O. Box 317
Tulbagh
6820

Tel: (0236) 30 0659
Fax: (0236) 30 0661

PADDAGANG & THEUNISKRAAL

Strolling down Tulbagh's historic Church Street you will reach Paddagang (froggy alley), housed in a quaint Cape Dutch building (1809) that was once a wine cellar. Paddagang produces a range of fine wines, all with amusing 'froggy' theme labels.

The picturesque setting, rolling lawns, sturdy oaks and rose garden, with the Winterhoek and Witzenberg mountain ranges forming the backdrop, combines with traditional Cape cuisine and local wines to create a memorable visit.

Friendly, smalltown hospitality, fresh wholesome country produce, *plattelandse* (country) dishes, a breathtaking setting and a selection of easy-drinking wines are guaranteed to make your visit to Paddagang an unforgettable experience.

BEVERAGES INCLUDE:
Paddasspring, Paddasang and Paddadundee (dry white), Platanna (semi-sweet), Paddarotti and Paddamanêl (dry red), Brulpadda Port, Paddagang Sherry, and Paddaqua (mineral water).

Theuniskraal, situated at the foot of the Winterhoek Mountains in the Tulbagh Valley, was established in 1705. Called Theuniskuyl until 1724, the farm was originally granted to Theunis Bevernagie in 1714, but has been in the hands of the Jordaan family since 1927.

In the late 1940s, Andries Jordaan, the father of the present owner, released his Theuniskraal Riesling and achieved one of the glowing moments in South Africa's oenological history when it was awarded the gold medal at the Commonwealth Wine Show in 1950. This wine was exported to London for many years, and is today, without doubt, the most sought-after Riesling in South Africa.

Since 1964, the estate has been jointly owned by the brothers Kobus (cellarmaster) and Rennie (viticulturist), whose son, Andries, ably assists in the cellar.

BEVERAGES INCLUDE:
Riesling, Semillon/Chardonnay, and a semi-sweet wine only available from the farm.

• Tours, tastings and sales by appointment.

Paddagang
Church Street
Tulbagh
6820

Tel: (0236) 30 0242
Fax: (0236) 30 0433

Theuniskraal
P.O. Box 34
Tulbagh
6820

Tel: (0236) 30 0690/30 0689
Fax: (0236) 30 1504

Worcester, the major centre of the Breede River Valley, is fondly referred to as the capital of the region.

A thriving commercial and industrial town, its economy is largely based on agriculture. The Breede River Valley is South Africa's largest wine producing region. It also produces the greatest volume of brandy and other spirits.

Worcester has become well known for its educational centres, especially the schools for the blind and the deaf. This is the only town in the country where traffic lights emit noises when the colours change, enabling the blind to cross the busy streets safely.

The attractions in and around the town are varied. The Open Air Living Museum at Kleinplasie offers a fascinating insight into the lifestyle of the early pioneers.

A flea market is held on Church Square every Saturday morning, and an Arts and Crafts Market every second Saturday at 43 Russell Street.

Worcester is an ideal base for scenic drives and the exploration of the surrounding areas, such as the Karoo National Botanical Garden, where the wonderful plants of the arid regions of South Africa can be seen.

The Karoo National Botanical Garden is situated approximately 2 km (1.2 miles) from the centre of the town of Worcester. During winter a series of bulbous plants and aloe species come into flower, culminating in a wonderful display of spring flowers that draws visitors from far and wide each year. The timing of this 'six-week spectacular' varies from year to year, but usually centres on September.

After October, when the displays are over, summer-flowering plants continue to attract the brilliant green sunbirds.

Indigenous plants are for sale daily. Guided tours for groups must be arranged in advance. Contact the curator on Tel: (0231) 7 0785.

The Hex River winds its way into the magnificent Hex River Valley, renowned for its splendid vineyards and top-quality grapes. The word *hex* is Dutch for witch, and legend tells of a witch who haunts the river below the mountain that separates the Western Cape from the plains of the Great Karoo.

The valley is at its most beautiful in autumn and early winter, when the snow-capped mountains compliment the brilliant scarlet of the balinka vines.

Worcester Winelands Association
P.O. Box 59
Worcester
6850

Tel: (023) 342-8710
Fax: (023) 342 2294

AAN-DE-DOORNS, BADSBERG & BERGSIG

A an-De-Doorns Co-op, 8 km (5 miles) outside Worcester on the Villiersdorp road has done well in the Veritas and Young Wine shows over the past few years, and is well known.

BEVERAGES INCLUDE:
Clairette Blanche, Chardonnay, Chenin Blanc, semi-sweet white wines, sparkling and fortified wines, red and white grape juice.

Opening times:
Weekdays: 08:00 – 17:00
• Cellar tours by appointment only.

Aan-De-Doorns Co-op Winery Ltd
P.O. Box 235
Worcester
6849

Tel: (023) 347 2301
Fax: (023) 347 4629

B adsberg, 1 km (0.6 miles) from the Goudini Spa, offers dry and semi-sweet white wine and grape juice.

BEVERAGES INCLUDE:
Chardonnay, Blanc de Blanc, Late Harvest, Hanepoot, Vin Sec, Rawson's Ruby Cabernet, and white grape juice.

Opening times:
Weekdays: 08:00 – 12:00 / 13:00 – 17:00
• Cellar tours held weekdays at 11:00.

Badsberg Co-operative Winery Ltd.
P.O. Box 72
Rawsonville
6845

Tel: (023) 349 1120
Fax: (023) 349 1122

I n the fertile Breede River Valley nestles Bergsig Wine Estate, where the Lategan family has been producing fine wines for six generations.

BEVERAGES INCLUDE:
Sauvignon Blanc, Chenin Blanc, Bouquet Light, Chardonnay, Weisser Riesling, Blanc de Noir, Gewürztraminer, Pinotage, sparkling wine, Cabernet Sauvignon Pinotage, Port, Hanepoot, and grape juice.

Opening times:
Weekdays: 08:00 – 17:00
Saturdays: 09:00 – 12:00
• Cellar tours/meals by arrangement.

Bergsig Estate
P.O. Box 15
Breerivier
6858

Tel: (023) 355 1603
Fax: (023) 355 1658

BOTHA CO-OP, BRANDVLEI & DE DOORNS

Located in the upper reaches of the Breede River Valley, some 20 km (12 miles) from Worcester on the Ceres road, Botha Co-op Wine Cellar lies in an area boasting a temperate climate and relatively high rainfall.

BEVERAGES INCLUDE:
Chardonnay, Hanepoot Jerepigo, Pinotage, Cabernet, Port, Sauvignon Blanc, dry and semi-sweet white wine, red wine, dessert wine, sparkling wine, and grape juice.

Opening times:
Weekdays: 08:00 – 12:30 / 13:30 – 17:30
Saturdays: 10:00 – 12:00
• Cellar tours by appointment only, about 20 people per group.

Botha Co-operative Winery
P.O. Box Botha
6857

Tel: (023) 355 1740
Fax: (023) 355 1615

Situated approximately 23 km (14 miles) from Worcester on the Villiersdorp road, Brandvlei Wine Cellar offers dry and semi-sweet white wines, red wine, dessert wine and grape juice.

BEVERAGES INCLUDE:
Dry red and white wines, Hanepoot, port, and red and white grape juice.

Opening times:
Weekdays: 08:00 – 12:30 / 13:30 – 17:30
• Cellar tours from Mondays to Fridays by appointment only.

Brandvlei Wine Cellar
P.O. Box 595
Worcester
6849

Tel/Fax: (023) 349 4215

De Doorns is situated about 30 km (18.6 miles) from Worcester on the N1 national route north.

BEVERAGES INCLUDE:
Chardonnay, Premier Grand Cru, Chenin Blanc, Colombar, Perlé Rosé and Blanc, Stein, Late Harvest, Roodehof, sparkling wine, sherry, hanepoot, and grape juice.

Opening times:
Weekdays: 08:30 – 12:30 / 13:30 – 17:00
• Cellar tours only during harvest (February – May), Tuesdays to Fridays.

De Doorns
P.O. Box 129
De Doorns, 6875

Tel: (023) 356 2835
Fax: (023) 356 2101

DE WET CO-OP & DU TOITSKLOOF

De Wet Co-operative Wine Cellar, founded on 15 April 1946, is the oldest cellar in the Worcester area. Originally, it produced about 3 000 tons of grapes per annum, but over the years developed into a quality cellar processing some 16 000–17 000 tons annually.

Since 1990, premium cultivars of red and white wine grapes have been planted on a large scale. To support this drive for higher quality, the Cellar has been modernised and has produced the champion red wine of the Worcester region several times during the past few years.

De Wet Co-operative is one of only two cellars producing a wine endorsed with the 'heart mark' of the South African Heart Foundation. Its Pettilant Fronte is a light, low-alcohol perlé wine, full of flavour but low in calories.

De Wet Co-operative Wine Cellar mainly supplies to the wholesale trade, but select wine is sold on the premises and in local restaurants.

BEVERAGES INCLUDE:
Sauvignon Blanc, Cape Riesling, Clairette Blanche, Fernão Pires, Blanc de Noir, Dry Red, semi-sweet and sweet wines, sparkling wine, and white sparkling grape juice.

Opening times:
Weekdays: 08:00 – 17:00
Saturdays: 09:00 – 12:00
• Cellar tours by appointment only on Wednesdays and Fridays.
• Mail orders dispatched daily.

De Wet Wine Cellar
P.O. Box 16
De Wet
6853

Tel: (023) 349 2710
Fax: (023) 349 2762

Du Toitskloof is situated about 29 km (18 miles) from Worcester on the N1 to Cape Town. It offers a range of wines, many of which have won acclaim nationally and internationally.

BEVERAGES INCLUDE:
Sauvignon Blanc, Riesling, Chardonnay, Chenin Blanc, Bukettraube, Blanc de Noir, Merlot, Pinotage, Shiraz, Cabernet Sauvignon, Blanc de Blanc, Late Vintage, sparkling wine, hanepoot, port, muscadel.

Opening times:
Weekdays: 08:30 – 12:30 / 13:30 – 17:00
• Cellar tours Mondays to Fridays, by appointment only.

Du Toitskloof Wine Cellar
P.O. Box 55
Rawsonville
6845

Tel: (023) 349 1601
Fax: (023) 349 1581

GOUDINI, GROOT EILAND & LATEGANSKOP

Goudini Wine Cellar lies some 10 km (6 miles) from Worcester. It offers dry and semi-sweet white wine, red wine, dessert wine and grape juice.

BEVERAGES INCLUDE:
Late Harvest Stein, Chenin Blanc, Clairette Blanche, Riesling, Umfiki (dry white), Chardonnay, Late Harvest, Grand Crû, Demi-Sec sparkling wine, Ruby Cabernet and Pinotage, white grape juice, and Hanepoot.

Opening times:
Weekdays: 08:30 – 12:00 / 13:30 – 17:00
• Cellar tours by appointment only.

Goudini Wine Cellar
P.O. Box 132
Rawsonville
6845

Tel: (023) 349 1090
Fax: (023) 349 1095

The Groot Eiland (big island) cellar is some 16 km (10 miles) from Worcester and 1 km (0.6 miles) from Rawsonville.

BEVERAGES INCLUDE:
Chardonnay, Sauvignon Blanc, Riesling, Chenin Blanc, Honigtraube, Sweet Hanepoot, Cabernet Sauvignon, as well as natural, sparkling grape juice.

Opening times:
Weekdays: 08:30 – 12:30 / 14:00 – 17:00
• Cellar tours Mondays to Fridays.

Groot Eiland Wine Cellar
P.O. Box 93
Rawsonville
6845

Tel: (023) 349 1140
Fax: (023) 349 1801

Lateganskop Wine Cellar is about 30 km (18.6 miles) from Worcester and supplies wine in bulk to wholesalers.

BEVERAGES INCLUDE:
Dry red and white wine, Hanepoot Jerepigo, White Jerepigo, and Port.

Opening times:
Weekdays: 08:00 – 17:00
• Mail orders welcome.

Lateganskop Wine Cellar
P.O. Box 44
Breerivier
6858

Tel/Fax: (023) 355 1719

LOUWSHOEK-VOORSORG, MERWIDA & NUY

Louwshoek-Voorsorg was founded in 1955. Today, some 13 500 tons of grapes are produced by 32 members, who still farm subdivisions of the original two farms, Dasboschrivier and Voorsorg.

BEVERAGES INCLUDE:
Chardonnay, Sauvignon Blanc, Riesling, dry red wines, Colombard and Late Harvest, dessert wines, and grape juice.

Opening times:
Weekdays: 08:30 – 12:30 / 13:30 – 17:00

Louwshoek-Voorsorg Wine Cellar
P.O. Box 174
Rawsonville
6845

Tel: (023) 349 1110
Fax: (023) 349 1980

Merwida, where manager-winemaker Wollie Wolhuter and winemaker Sarel van Staden preside, lies 10 km (6 miles) from Worcester.

BEVERAGES INCLUDE:
Riesling, Chardonnay, Sauvignon Blanc, Chenin Blanc, Cuvée Brût, Ruby Cabernet, Port, red and white grape juice.

Opening times:
Weekdays: 08:30 – 12:00 / 13:30 – 17:30
• Cellar tours by appointment only.

Merwida Wine Cellar
P.O. Box 4
Rawsonville
6845

Tel: (023) 349 1144
Fax: (023) 349 1953

Nuy Wine Cellar, at the foot of the Langeberg Mountains, is one of the smaller co-operative cellars in South Africa and has been the domain of winemaker Wilhelm Linde since 1971.

Nuy wins top prizes at local and national wine shows. The coveted Diners' Club Award was presented to Wilhelm Linde in 1988 and 1991.

BEVERAGES INCLUDE:
Full range of dry and off-dry white wines, Rouge de Nuy, muscadel and grape juice.

Opening times:
Weekdays: 08:30 – 16:30
Saturdays: 08:30 – 12:30

Nuy Wine Cellar
P.O. Box 5225
Worcester
6851

Tel: (023) 347 0272
Fax: (023) 347 4994

OPSTAL, OVERHEX & ROMANSRIVER

The Opstal Estate Cellar is about 29 km (18 miles) from Worcester in the Slanghoek Valley.

BEVERAGES INCLUDE:
Dry and semi-sweet white wines, Hanepoot.

Opening times:
Weekdays: 09:00 – 11:00 / 14:00 – 17:00
• Cellar/farm tours: Mondays, Wednesdays and Fridays by appointment only.

Opstal Estate Wine Cellar Ltd.
P.O. Box 27
Rawsonville
6845

Tel: (023) 349 1066
Fax: (023) 349 1801

The Overhex Wine Cellar is situated 6 km (3.7 miles) from Worcester on the Robertson Road. Over the past three years the cellar has undergone dynamic changes, making it well worth a visit.

BEVERAGES INCLUDE:
Chardonnay, Sauvignon Blanc, Chenin Blanc, Colombar, Late Harvest, Vin Rouge, Muscadel, sparkling wine, and grape juice.

Opening times:
Weekdays: 08:00 – 17:00
Saturdays: 09:00 – 12:00
• Cellar tours by appointment only.

Overhex Wine Cellar
P.O. Box 139
Worcester
6849

Tel: (023) 347 5012
Fax: (023) 347 1057

Romansriver Co-operative Wine Cellar, some 40 km (25 miles) from Worcester, offers a full range of wine and grape products.

BEVERAGES INCLUDE:
Ceres Vin Blanc, Colombard, Grand Crû, Chenin Blanc, Sauvignon Blanc, Chardonnay, Vin Rood, Cabernet Sauvignon, and red and white grape juices.

Opening times:
Weekdays: 08:00 – 17:00
Saturdays: 08:30 – 10:00
• Cellar tours by appointment only.
• Mail orders welcome.

Romansriver Co-operative
Wine Cellar Ltd.
P.O. Box 108
Wolseley
6830

Tel: (0236) 31 1070/80
Fax: (0236) 31 1102

SLANGHOEK, VILLIERSDORP & WABOOMSRIVIER

Slanghoek Co-operative Wine Cellar Ltd, founded in 1951, enjoys a picturesque setting with prolific vegetation and charming waterfalls in winter.

Thanks to its geographic situation its wines have a unique character.

BEVERAGES INCLUDE:
Dry red and white wines, Special Late Harvest, sparkling and dessert wines, and juices.

Opening times:
Mondays to Thursdays: 07:30 – 12:30 / 13:30 – 17:30
Fridays: 07:30 – 12:30 / 13:30 – 16:30
• Cellar tours by appointment only.

Slanghoek Wine Cellar
P.O. Box 75
Rawsonville
6845

Tel: (023) 349 3026
Fax: (023) 349 3157

Villiersdorp Cellar, 50 km (31 miles) from Worcester, has a full range of wines and grape juice in its wine tasting centre, Kelkiewyn, which also houses a farm stall and a little coffee shop.

BEVERAGES INCLUDE:
White wine blends, red and white wines, sparkling and dessert wines, grape juice.

Opening times:
Weekdays: 08:30 – 17:00
Saturdays: 08:30 – 13:00
• Cellar tours by prior arrangement.

Villiersdorp Cellar
P.O. Box 466
Durbanville
7551

Tel: (028) 840 1151
Fax: (028) 840 1833

Waboomsrivier is presently overseen by winemaker Chris van der Merwe. The cellar has 47 members.

BEVERAGES INCLUDE:
Riesling, Chenin Blanc, Grand Crû, Perlé wines, Ruby Cabernet, Pinotage, Cinsaut.

Opening times:
Weekdays: 08:00 – 17:00
Saturdays: 08:00 – 10:00
• Cellar tours from Mondays to Fridays.

Waboomsrivier Wine Cellar
P.O. Box 24
Breerivier
6858

Tel: (023) 355 1730
Fax: (023) 355 1731

Only an hour and a half from Cape Town by car, and adorned by the Breede River and the beautiful Langeberg Mountains, the Robertson Valley is becoming a popular getaway haven. It embraces the districts of Ashton, Bonnievale, McGregor and Robertson, each with their own charm and history.

The valley is blessed with an ideal environment for vineyards and this, combined with sophisticated viticulture and cellar techniques and a serious commitment to quality by the local wine producers, has resulted in numerous international and local awards. The area has, over the last decade, gained an enviable reputation as a producer of excellent white and red wines, as well as Cap Classique and fortified wines.

This is also the first region to launch a generic wine, Sinnya Valley (*sinnya* is the Khoisan word for the Breede River Valley). Following huge success in the export market, this wine was subsequently launched in South Africa.

The wineries are all situated close to one another and offer the warmest hospitality. Of the 31 wineries, 21 are open to the public – tastings at all of these are free of charge.

A range of excellent restaurants and informal eateries is available. And for entertainment there are antique and arts-and-craft shops to explore, and farm stalls selling fresh produce. Scenic hiking and bridle trails are offered by the Vrolijkheid

Nature Reserve and the Pat Busch Private Reserve.

The Robertson Valley celebrates several annual festivals that have become popular pilgrimages for wine, nature and fun lovers. At the Food and Wine Festival in October the visitor can enjoy delicious wines and traditional fare, and purchase Robertson Valley wines at farm prices.

Accommodation ranges from inns in quaint country towns to cottages on stud farms, among orchards and vineyards, on the banks of the Breede River, or in nature reserves. Here the visitor can experience traditional country hospitality.

Robertson Valley Wine Route
P.O. Box 550
Robertson
6705

Tel:(02351) 3167
Fax: (02351) 5079

Ashton Tourism Bureau
Tel: (0234) 5 1100
Bonnievale Tourism Bureau
Tel: (02346) 2105
McGregor Tourism Bureau
Tel: (02353) 954
Robertson Tourism Bureau
Tel: (02351) 4437

BON COURAGE

Where the Klaas Voogds and Breede rivers join lies Bon Courage with its serene, old Cape Dutch homestead built in 1818. Originally, the estate was part of the farm Goedemoed which had been acquired by the Dutch Reformed Church in the 1920s.

In 1927 the subdivided property was put up for auction and the highest bidder for the largest piece was Willie Bruwer, who replanted the whole estate with steen and muscadel grapes, vinifying and fortifying the juice and selling the product in bulk to the KWV.

Willie's youngest son, André, the present owner, majored in wine making at Elsenburg Agricultural College and settled on the farm in 1965.

His introduction of computerised drip irrigation in 1972 and the modernisation of the cellar in 1974 geared the estate into a thoughtfully managed wine-producing operation. In 1980 André purchased a neighbouring farm, registered his property as an estate and renamed it Bon Courage (French for Goedemoed) in 1983.

In 1986 André started night harvesting and three years later he imported a mechanical harvester from France. In 1990 André's eldest son, Jacques, who also graduated at the Elsenburg Agricultural College, joined him on the farm. The purchase of yet another neighbouring farm enlarged the estate to 175 ha (432 acres).

The many awards, trophies, double gold and gold medals won at various wine shows since 1983, testify to the quality of the estate's wines.

BEVERAGES INCLUDE:
Cape Riesling, Chardonnay, Sauvignon Blanc, Rhine Riesling, Bouquet Light, Bouquet Blanc, Le Bouquet, Blanc de Noir, Gewürztraminer Special Late Harvest, Muscadel, Noble Late Harvest, Shiraz, sparkling wines, and Vin Sec & Vin Doux.

Opening times:
Weekdays: 08:00 – 17:00
Saturdays: 09:00 – 12:30

Bon Courage Wine Estate
P.O. Box 589
Robertson
6705

Tel: (02351) 4178
Fax: (02351) 3581
http://www.interads.co.za

BONNIEVALE CO-OP & CLAIRVAUX

Bonnievale Co-op, formed in 1964 by 29 members, is the largest winery in the Bonnievale district. While the first harvest in 1965 produced only 4 613 tons, the yearly grape intake increased to a current 12 500 tons produced by 61 members in the Robertson, Bonnievale, Buffeljagsrivier and Swellendam areas, allowing the cellar to produce wine from various cultivars.

Gerrit van Zyl joined the cellar as manager-winemaker in 1993. He is a respected wine taster, a member of the tasting panel at the National Young Wine Show and also serves on the certification board of the Robertson Valley.

During 1995, the cellar entered its product in the National Young Wine Show for the first time and received an award for each of its 10 entries.

BEVERAGES INCLUDE:
Dry and off-dry white, Late Harvest, red and dessert wine, and white grape juice.

Opening times:
Weekdays: 08:00 – 17:00

Kapteinsdrift, Bonnievale
P.O. Box 6730
Bonnievale
6730

Tel: (02346) 2795/2359
Fax: (02346) 2332

Clairvaux, nestled in the folds of the Robertson valley, is a special place where winemaker and the elements unite their energies to create a range of truly unique wines.

The estate underwent change and renewal in 1995 when it was decided to establish its product on the national as well as international markets. Cellarmaster, Kobus van der Merwe, has produced a number of Veritas award-winning wines since then.

A variety of grape juices are also produced here, and Sparkles is a non-alcoholic beverage with the same taste and character as real sparkling wine.

BEVERAGES INCLUDE:
Sauvignon Blanc, Chenin Blanc, Rhine Riesling, Stein, Soleil, Ruby Cabernet, Red Jerepigo, Golden Jerepigo, Port, and Hopp Johanna.

Opening times:
Weekdays: 08:00 – 17:30
Saturdays: 09:00 – 12:30

Clairvaux Wines
P.O. Box 179
Robertson
6705

Tel: (02351) 3843/61130
Fax: (02351) 61925

GOEDVERWACHT

The estate of Goedverwacht is situated in the Breede River Valley in the Robertson District. Its owners, the Du Toit brothers, Thys and wine-maker Jan, have approximately 100 ha (247 acres) under vines, producing in the region of 11 000 l (19 360 pints) per hectare.

Although this is substantially lower than the actual capability of the vines, Jan maintains that it is part of their success. Another factor comes into play during the harvesting season which begins in mid-January: grapes are only picked early in the mornings while it is still cool. Considerations like these, combined with a favourable climate, noble vines and careful supervision have culminated in wines that are loved and talked about.

For many years Goedverwacht produced solely for South Africa's leading wholesaler. In 1993, however, the Du Toit brothers decided to enter into the export market under their own label. As a result the Goedverwacht Sauvignon Blanc, as well as the unwooded and wooded Chardonnay are acclaimed, both nationally and internationally.

BEVERAGES INCLUDE:
Goedverwacht Colombar, Sauvignon Blanc, and wooded and unwooded Chardonnay.

• Tasting and sales by appointment.

Goedverwacht
Thys Du Toit & Sons cc
P.O. Box 128
Bonnievale
6730

Tel/Fax: (02346) 3430

GRAHAM BECK WINES

The name Madeba was given to the estate by its previous owners who bought the farm in 1935. Madeba means 'place of running water' and refers to the Biblical town that was situated on the old King's Highway (now in modern Jordan).

When Graham Beck bought the farm in 1983, he did not know that another Madiba (the tribal term of endearment for South African State President Nelson Mandela) was destined to change the course of South African history.

Cellar I was built in 1990 specifically for the production of *Méthode champenoise* wines and is extremely practical in design, ensuring minimum handling and movement of the wine. Cellar II was commissioned in 1991 for the production of red and white table wines, which represent the best grapes from each vintage under the Madeba Cellar range. This cellar's capacity is being enlarged to 3 444 tons. Cellar III houses the packaging component of Graham Beck Wines.

In recent years, 160 ha (395 acres) of vineyard were replanted and upgraded. The vineyards are irrigated by means of a fully integrated computerised system. Tensiometers that measure moisture stress levels in the soil were installed to optimise the irrigation systems.

Madeba Farm is situated in a valley that is bisected by the Breede and Finch rivers. The three state-of-the-art cellars at Madeba are as unique as the farm itself. They provide a fresh and fascinating rendition of avant-garde architecture: the orange walls and long, curved, green roof blend extremely well into the surrounding landscape, while the interior richly reflects the deep purple of the vygie's delicate flower, the dark green of the fynbos and orange of the sand and soil of the Klein Karoo.

The 800 ha (1 977 acres) of indigenous fynbos adjacent to the vineyards have become home to buck, zebra, ostrich and a variety of birds.

BEVERAGES INCLUDE:
Brût, Brût Blanc de Blanc, Chardonnay, Sauvignon Blanc, Railroad Red, Waterside White, and Bouquet Blanc.

Opening times:
Weekdays: 09:00 – 17:00
Saturdays: 09:00 – 13:00

Graham Beck Wines
P.O. Box 724
Robertson
6705

Tel: (02351) 61214
Fax: (02351) 5164

MCGREGOR WINERY

Founded in 1861, the village of Mcgregor, named after the Reverend Andrew McGregor, who settled and ministered in the Robertson district, is an enchanting example of the Cape's Victorian heritage. Little whitewashed cottages lean together in a neighbourly fashion, windows shuttered against the sun and thatch sagging slightly under the weight of years. Pumpkins ripen on rooftops and purple bougainvillea blooms frame painted doors, dogs yawn and scratch in the midday heat and children play companionably in the sand – colours seem deeper and vines greener.

Here you will find the McGregor winery. A pristine-white, classical Cape façade decorates a cellar that has adapted to the high-tech demands of the '90s, replacing open concrete *kuipe* (wooden vats) with gleaming stainless steel tanks, concentrating on a smaller range of high-quality wines, and breaking new ground as a class winner on the SA Young Wine Show.

Winemaker Danie Marais' first harvest at McGregor in 1994, was a record of over 10 000 tons, with a concurrent upgrade in quality. He has ensured that the Scottish links are reflected in the elegant McGregor wine label.

BEVERAGES INCLUDE:
Sauvignon Blanc, Chenin Blanc, Colombard/Chardonnay, Vrolijkheid, Colombard, Late Harvest, sparkling wine, *Village Red, Red Muscadel, White Muscadel, and grape juice.*

Opening times:
Weekdays: 08:00 – 12:30 / 13:30 – 17:00
Saturdays: 09:00 – 12:30

McGregor Winery
Private Bag X 619
McGregor
6708

Tel: (02353) 741
Fax: (02353) 829

MERWESPONT

The piece of land on which Merwespont cellar was built in 1955, was bought for 50 pounds from Laubsher van der Merwe.

From humble beginnings, Merwespont has developed into a winery set to launch itself into the big time. To date, it has been known primarily as a white wine producer with Chenin Blanc and Colombard predominating. The winery earned an award for the best white wine at the 1989 South African National Young Wine Show.

Conditions are suitable for the production of quality wine, offering the variety of the warm low-lying banks of the Breede River and the cooler slopes of the Langeberg. Vines are further cooled by the southeaster, funnelled in from the coast through the mouth formed by the Langeberg and Riviersonderend mountain ranges. Hence the move toward premium varieties like Chardonnay and Sauvignon Blanc, Cabernet Sauvignon and Shiraz.

Production equipment and facilities have been modernised, four bag presses and several drainers have been installed over the past two years, and the grape intake area has been upgraded. The wines are fruit-driven and made for immediate enjoyment.

BEVERAGES INCLUDE:
The Merwespont range consists of Cabernet Sauvignon, Columbar Chardonnay and

Chardonnay (unwooded). The Mont Vue range offers Blanc de Blanc, Vin Rosé, Late Vintage, Hanepoot and grape juice.

Opening times:
Weekdays: 08:00 –12:30 / 13:30 – 17:00
Saturdays: By appointment only.
• Cellar tours by appointment during harvest.
• Wine tours by appointment from mid-January to the end of March.

Merwespont
P.O. Box 68
Bonnievale
6730

Tel: (02346) 2800
Fax: (02346) 2734

NORDALE WINERY

Nordale Wine Cellar was established on 30 June 1950 with nine founder members. In those days the total yield was sold as rebate wine for distillation, but since cold fermentation was introduced in 1965 and the vineyards were upgraded with noble cultivars, a significant portion of the harvest has been used for wine making.

The cultivars received at this cellar include chenin blanc, colombard, chardonnay, sauvignon blanc, muscadel, chenel and emeral riesling. It didn't take long for the Nordale wines to find their way into the collections of connoisseurs.

Robertson Valley has been blessed with consistent summer temperatures of 20–21°C (68–70°F), an average annual rainfall of about 250 mm (10 inches) and light humidity, which are counteracted by cool evenings and gentle breezes. The colder Klein Karoo winter nights ensure healthy vines, while the rich alluvial soil along the banks of the Breede River, and the fairly compact clay and shale of the higher reaches also play an important role in the production of fine wines.

One reason for Nordale's success lies with its winemaker, Emile Schoch. This BSc graduate in Agriculture and former KWV wine expert is also an accomplished wine taster, a man of few words and many talents who, with typical modesty, describes his own handiwork as 'easy drinking wines'.

The greatest challenge for any cellar wishing to compete on the export markets of the world is to ensure that consistent superior quality of its product always provides an edge on its competitors. For this reason, Nordale's production planning programme includes the regular upgrading of its cellar equipment with the very best modern technology has to offer.

BEVERAGES INCLUDE:
Chardonnay, Colombar, Late Harvest, Vin Rouge, Muscadel Jerepigo, and red and white grape juice.

Opening times:
Mondays to Thursdays: 08:00 – 17:00
Fridays: 07:30 – 16:30
• Closed over weekends.

Nordale Winery
P.O. Box 105
Bonnievale
6730

Tel: (02346) 2050
Fax: (02346) 2192

ROBERTSON WINERY

Valleys steeped in sunshine, low rainfall and cool sea breezes at night create a perfect climate for the healthy vines and rich, fruity grapes that give these wines the distinctive character and fine reputation for which Robertson Winery is renowned.

Established in 1941, Robertson Winery is not only the oldest Co-op in the valley, but also one of the biggest in the country. The winery's first wine-maker, the late Pon van Zyl, was known as 'the father of Colombard' in South Africa, having instigated the making of Colombard to a great extent.

He was succeeded by Bowen Botha, who now manages the cellar with two additional winemakers. The 42 farmer-members deliver approximately 25 000 tons of grapes annually, to produce some 25 million litres (44 million pints) of wine! The cellar is situated in Robertson itself, where the outstanding and quite extensive range, which has won numerous awards and medals, is made, bottled and sold. The winery also boasts the first (and, to date, only) aseptic carton packaging plant, the Combibloc, which produces fine wines in quality, affordable packaging.

BEVERAGES INCLUDE:
Columbard, Sauvignon Blanc, Chardonnay, Chardonnay Sauvignon Blanc, Columbard Chardonnay, Beaukeit, Late Harvest, Rheingold, Cabernet Sauvignon, Merlot, Robertson Ruby Cabernet, Muscadel,

sparkling wine like Santino Vin Sec, Vin Doux and Spumante, and grape juice. There is a Rob Roy range of 5 l (8.8 pint) casks of wine, as well as a select range of wines in 500 ml cartons.

Opening times:
Mondays to Thursdays: 08:00 – 17:00
Fridays: 08:00 – 16:30
Saturdays: 09:00 – 13:00
• Cellar tours can be arranged on request.

Robertson Winery
P.O. Box 37
Robertson
6705

Tel: (02351) 3059/61703
Fax: (02351) 2926

ROODEZANDT WINERY

Roodezandt was founded on 18 September 1953 and has a long and colourful history that dates back far beyond the 40 years of its existence.

The winery was established by the farmers who delivered their grapes to the old Sonskyn Winery, which in turn hired the building from the Robertson Distillery. Building, machinery and grounds were eventually taken over by Roodezandt, which was established on 18 September 1953.

The name Roodezandt, which was accepted in a meeting on 22 January 1954, came from the farm's original name 'Over het Roodezandt' which had incorporated the first plots of Robertson town.

Roodezandt presently has 52 members distributed over a 30 km (18-mile) radius. It handles 23 000 tons of grapes per annum, but in spite of the big volume the emphasis falls on quality. The bulk of the wines are sold to wholesale merchants, but Roodezandt also sells a top range of bottled wines at the cellar.

BEVERAGES INCLUDE:
Sparkling wines, Colombard, Sauvignon Blanc, Chardonnay, Special Late Harvest, Roodehuiswyn, Cabernet Sauvignon, dessert wines, grape juice, and Vino Zanté white wine.

Opening times:
Weekdays: 08:00 – 17:30
Saturdays: 09:00 – 12:30

• Cellar tours by appointment during pressing season only.

Roodezandt Winery
P.O. Box 164
Robertson
6705

Tel: (02351) 61160
Fax: (02351) 5074

Rooiberg was established in April 1964 by 11 farmers under the chairmanship of Mr H.A. Conradie. From the beginning, the cellar's philosophy was to make good quality wine, rather than have distilling wine as its base like so many other cellars at the time. The winery took in its first grapes in 1965. Today, 34 members contribute from individual farms around the cellar, which crushes in excess of 14 000 tons.

Winemaker Tommy Loftus is quick to credit the cellar's successes to its grape growers. Proper planning regarding new varieties, soils, gradients, irrigation and micro-climates has led to an amazing hit rate since the early '70s and Rooiberg has been top achiever in the Robertson area since the inception of Bottled Wine Shows in South Africa.

Achievements include 10 double gold medals up to 1990 and several Veritas awards from 1991 onwards. These achievements continued up to 1996, when Rooiberg had the honour of winning 6 double gold and 6 gold medals. In total, this Robertson-based winery has achieved 14 double gold and 36 gold medals in the six years since the inception of Veritas, and has also received various international awards.

The production cellar at Rooiberg recently underwent a R3.5 million upgrade. The new, improved technology, coupled with detailed varietal planning and top-quality grapes augurs well for even more enjoyable wines in the future.

BEVERAGES INCLUDE:
Brût, Demi-Sec, Vin Doux and alcohol free sparkling wine; white wines like Chardonnay, Riesling, Colombard, Bukettraube and Late Vintage; red wines include Roodewyn, Pinotage, Shiraz and Cabernet Sauvignon; also dessert wines and white grape juice.

Opening times:
Weekdays: 08:00 – 17:30
Saturdays: 08:00 – 13:00
• Orders accepted through the post or telephonically
• Cellar tours by appointment only.

Rooiberg Winery
P.O. Box 358
Robertson
6705

Tel: (02351) 61663/4
Fax: (02351) 3295

SPRINGFIELD ESTATE

In late 1995, Springfield Estate, situated on the Breede River in the Robertson Valley (an hour and a half by car from Cape Town) proudly made its wines available to the public for the first time. However, Abrie and his father, Piet, have decades of wine making experience, having supplied a major producer for over thirty years.

Since their public release, Springfield's range of wines has been hailed by various of South Africa's top wine writers. Abrie Bruwer further excelled himself by producing a 1996 Veritas double gold winner: his 1996 Sauvignon Blanc Special Cuvée. This latest addition to the range is Abrie's *pièce de resistance*. Grapes from the estate's prime sauvignon blanc vineyard were specially nurtured on the vine, during harvesting and in the cellar. Abrie is deservedly proud of this achievement which bears testimony to his dedication and passionate striving for excellence.

In his determination to produce wines of the utmost quality, Abrie has modernised his cellar by importing some of the most up-to-date equipment available in Europe. The farm's unique terroir, combined with Abrie's wine making skills, ensure distinct and individual wines. Vines are purposefully kept 'low-yielding' and picked in the cool nights characteristic of the area. The cold chain is continued into the temperature-controlled cellar.

Abrie Bruwer is delighted to personally show visitors around the farm and cellar.

BEVERAGES INCLUDE:
Special Cuvée (Sauvignon Blanc), Chardonnay, Sauvignon Blanc, Colombard/Chardonnay, and Cabernet Sauvignon.

Opening times:
Mondays to Saturdays: 08:00 – 17:00

Springfield Estate
P.O. Box 770
Robertson
6705

Tel: (02351) 3661
Fax: (02351) 3664

VAN LOVEREN

Home to three generations of the Retief family, the brothers Nico and Wynand have already been joined by Nico's sons, Hennie and Bussell. Wynand's sons, Phillip and Neil, will be next to join the family estate.

The original farm was bought in 1937 and renamed after Christina van Loveren, an ancestor of Jean Retief (mother of Nico and Wynand), who came to South Africa in 1692. Christina's beautiful bridal chest, already 300 years old, still has a special place in the homestead.

Winemakers Wynand and Bussell Retief produce 21 different wines in their modern cellar. These wines have won an enviable reputation of consistent superiority, and Van Loveren's beverages regularly feature as top selection of the various wine tasting clubs.

The beautiful garden surrounding the Van Loveren cellar, homestead and tasting room has become synonymous with the quality of the estate's wines. Its splendour is a result of the dedication of Jean Retief. For eight months of the year the property is distinctly marked by scarlet cannas growing along the roadside.

Visitors to Van Loveren are invited to walk through the idyllic garden and to taste the wines at the rondawel under the beautiful trees.

BEVERAGES INCLUDE:
Chardonnay, Sauvignon Blanc, Rhine Riesling, Colombar, Colombar/Chardonnay, Colombar/Sauvignon Blanc, Cape Riesling, Special Late Harvest Gewürztraminer, Red Muscadel, two unique Blanc de Noirs – one made from Red Muscadel, the other from Shiraz Van Loveren River Red – Cabernet Sauvignon/Shiraz, Hungarian Hárslevelü, Portuguese Fernão Pires, Pinot Gris, Brût, Demi-Sec, and Vin Doux.

Opening times:
Weekdays: 08:30 – 17:00
Saturdays: 09:30 – 13:00

Van Loveren
P.O. Box 19
Klaasvoogds
6707

Tel: (0234) 5 1505
Fax: (0234) 5 1336

174 THE ROBERTSON VALLEY

VAN ZYLSHOF ESTATE

The Van Zyl family has been producing wine on the Van Zylshof Estate, situated near Bonnievale in the southern part of the Robertson wine region, for 3 generations. The white wines, made by the father-and-son team of Chris and Andri van Zyl, have become household names in South Africa and internationally.

The estate consists of about 35 ha (84 acres) of lime-rich soil on a gentle southern slope above the Breede River. Some 26 ha (64 acres) of the total area are currently under vineyards.

The deep, rich soil and moderate climate influenced by the Breede River and cooling breezes from the Atlantic Ocean, create perfect conditions for the cultivation of the chardonnay and sauvignon blanc varieties.

Since 1984, the Van Zyls have concentrated on planting only the best clones available of these two cultivars and have already been awarded a gold medal for the Sauvignon Blanc. The first chardonnay was pressed in 1995.

The small estate concentrates on limited quantities of high-quality hand-made wines. A combination of the time-honoured methods with modern technology brings out the very best in the grapes, both in the vineyards and in the cellar.

BEVERAGES INCLUDE:
Chenin Blanc, Sauvignon Blanc, Riverain (unwooded Chardonnay), Chardonnay.

• The estate is open for tastings by appointment only.

Van Zylshof Estate
P.O. Box 64
Bonnievale
6730

Tel: (02346) 2940
Fax: (02346) 3503

WELTEVREDE WINE ESTATE

Weltevrede, meaning 'well satisfied', is a wine estate whose proud heritage stretches back over many years, and where the art of wine making has been passed on, from generation to generation, since 1912.

The wine making tradition of the Jonker family began when Klaas Jonker purchased the farm which was then just scrub land and planted the first vineyards in the area. He was followed by Japie Jonker, who in 1933, began wine farming on Weltevrede. Today, the tradition is carried on by current owner, Lourens Jonker, who since his days as an Air Force pilot, has always set his sights high. Lourens's son, Philip, joined him at the beginning of 1997.

In 1975, this was the first estate in the valley to bottle its own wine, Weltevrede Colombard, followed in 1976 by South Africa's first certified Red Muscadel. In 1977, the first Muscat de Hambourg, which was also the first dessert wine offered at the Nederburg Auction, was bottled here. In 1979, the Bonnievale district's first certified Wine of Origin was bottled, followed by one of the first South African white wines, Privé du Bois, matured in small French oak casks. 1983 saw the Breede River Valley's first Gewürztraminer and South Africa's first Therona wine in 1986. Year after year, Weltevrede's wines have been acclaimed for their quality, winning numerous trophies and gold and double gold Veritas awards.

The folks at Weltevrede invite you to visit the estate, tour the cellar and get a first-hand glimpse of the fascinating process of wine making. Round off your visits with a delicious meal, accompanied by one of the outstanding wines, in the restaurant.

For visitors wishing to stay awhile, Ons Huisie (our house) is a self-contained chalet that offers accommodation for two people.

BEVERAGES INCLUDE:
Philip Jonker Brût (méthode Cap Classique), Cape Riesling, wood-matured Privé du Bois and Chardonnay; off-dry Rhine Riesling, Gewürztraminer and Blanc de Noir, white muscadel and white grape juice.

Opening times:
Weekdays: 08:30 – 17:00
Saturdays: 09:00 – 15:30
• Restaurant open during the holidays.

Weltevrede Wine Estate
P.O. Box 6
Bonnievale
6730

Tel: (02346) 2141/2/6
Fax: (02346) 2460

ZANDVLIET WINE ESTATE

Lovely, historic Zandvliet Estate, with its stately Cape Dutch homestead, beautiful rose garden and thoroughbred racehorses, has been regarded as one of South Africa's top Shiraz producers for the past 20 years, under the guidance of winemaker Paul de Wet.

In 1870, Paul's great-grandfather, JS de Wet, purchased the farm and developed it into an ostrich and wine farm. Later, Paul's father set about making Zandvliet into a model stud farm (which bred a number of Durban July winners). Paul de Wet's BSc in agriculture from Stellenbosch University, was augmented by a culture of perfection in the vineyards and the cellar, instilled in him at a young age by his father.

The estate's 1976 Shiraz, as well as the following four vintages, were the first produced outside the traditional red wine areas to receive the 'superior' rating. The 1992 Shiraz was awarded a Veritas double gold.

After 27 years of producing Shiraz, and subsequently Cabernet Sauvignon and Chardonnay, Paul believes that the most important element that sets Zandvliet apart from the rest is the quality of their soils. Cellar techniques are kept straightforward. A temperature-controlled barrel fermentation cellar was built three years ago. Wines are aged in new and old French oak barrels and experimentation has begun with American white oak.

In 1994 the Astonvale label was produced for the export market with great success, and was subsequently launched on the local market.

The classical façade of the tasting room at Zandvliet Estate looks out onto a cool oak-covered garden. Tastings are not charged for. Bed-and-breakfast accommodation is available at a cottage on the estate.

BEVERAGES INCLUDE:
Zandvliet Chardonnay; Astonvale range – Chardonnay, Sauvignon Blanc, Colombard, Crême, Blanc Fumé, Chenin Blanc/Sauvignon Blanc; Zandvliet Shiraz, Zandvliet Cabernet, Zandvliet Sauvignon; Astonvale range – Shiraz, Sauvignon, and Shiraz/Cabernet.

Opening times:
Weekdays: 09:00 – 17:00
Saturdays: 09:00 – 13:00

Zandvliet Wine Estate
P.O. Box 36
Ashton
6715

Tel: (0234) 5 1146
Fax: (0234) 5 1327

The Klein Karoo is a place of extraordinary vistas, where austere ridges and sharp peaks frame lush valleys dotted with small hamlets.

Wine culture was established in the Klein Karoo, also known as Kannaland, during the 18th century, when casks of heady brandy accompanied transport wagons on their pioneering journeys into the interior.

Today's Klein Karoo Wine Route stretches from Cogmanskloof outside Montagu, in the west, as far as the hamlet of De Rust in the east, and produces pleasant, fruity wines that reflect the strong contrasts of this region.

The charming towns of the Klein Karoo are a reminder of an era past.

The streets of **Calitzdorp**, which overlooks the Gamka River valley, are abuzz every July when the local port festival draws crowds who want to enjoy the wine tasting, arts and crafts and the famous marathon, where the winner's prize is his, or her, weight in port.

The spa, some 20 km (12 miles) from town, is one of the biggest attractions of the area, and visitors come to relax and unwind in the thermal mineral baths.

For nature lovers there is the **Gamka Mountain Nature Reserve**, which has various trails ranging from day walks to a two-day conducted hike.

Barrydale, situated in a fertile fruit and rose growing valley, is surrounded by majestic mountains that reflect a kaleidoscope of colours at sunset.

Oudtshoorn, the capital of the Klein Karoo, is a large town that offers a range of activities and accommodation facilities. Warm, dry summers and sunny winter days make this ideal ostrich country. A number of the ostrich farms in the area offer guided tours and the unique opportunity to ride the big birds.

There is also a butterfly farm and the Cango Crocodile Ranch where over 300 crocodiles and a variety of snakes are on view. Cheetahland is a special enclosure within the ranch which houses the world's tamest cheetahs.

The Cango Caves, 26 km (16 miles) north of Oudtshoorn, are one of Africa's most spectacular natural wonders. They consist of 28 massive caverns filled with fascinating limestone formations and are open to the public all year round, except Christmas Day.

De Rust is a pretty Victorian village flanked by the Swartberg Mountains. Its renowned attraction is Meiringspoort, one of South Africa's most impressive mountain passes – the winding road crosses the same stream no less than 26 times.

Oudtshoorn Tourism Bureau
P.O. Box 255
Oudtshoorn
6620

Tel: (0442) 29 2532
Fax: (0442) 22 8226

BOPLAAS ESTATE

Grapes for wine and brandy have been grown on Boplaas for over 150 years. Boplaas is a family concern for Carel Nel, the owner and winemaker, who is a Cape Wine Master.

Danie Nel, great-grandfather of Carel Nel, had exported brandy to London way back in 1880. After new distillation licences were recently granted, Boplaas became the first private cellar in the country to release a certified potstill brandy. This brandy was chosen for a state banquet hosted by President Mandela for German Federal Chancellor, Dr. Helmut Kohl.

Although port and brandy made a name for Boplaas, the modern cellar also produces a range of outstanding table wines. For the past seven years Boplaas has been the champion cellar at the Southern Cape Bottled Wine Show, and the Boplaas Chardonnay was chosen by the biggest German wine magazine *Alles über Wein*, as the best from South Africa.

Port is the flagship wine of Boplaas, and on various occasions has been crowned South African Champion, also having been selected for first-class flights on the national airways. Only traditional Portuguese cultivars are used to produce a range which includes White, Ruby, Vintage, Vintage Reserve and late-bottled Vintage Port. A small percentage of grapes are purchased from selected Stellenbosch vineyards, to supplement the estate's table wines.

Great attention is paid to environmentally friendly farming practices and, as a result, a great number of garden birds, guineafowl, partridges and occasional otters and wild buck may be spotted on the farm.

Boplaas produces a range of tasty dry fruit chips (*happies*), and Bushman artifacts are on display in the tasting room.

BEVERAGES INCLUDE:
Sauvignon Blanc, Chardonnay, Merlot, Cabernet Sauvignon, Pinotage, Golden Harvest, and an excellent range of port.

Opening times:
Weekdays: 08:00 – 17:00
Saturdays: 09:00 – 15:00
• Cellar tours and lunches for groups can be arranged in advance.

Boplaas Estate
P.O. Box 156
Calitzdorp
6660

Tel: (044) 213 3326
Fax: (044) 213 3750

DIE KRANS ESTATE

Die Krans, famous for its excellent quality port, is situated between the vineyards in the upper reaches of the picturesque Gamka River Valley.

The history of the estate dates back to 1890, when the farm Die Krans was bought by the Nel family. The present cellar was built in 1964 and in 1979 it became the first estate wine cellar in the Klein Karoo.

Die Krans has won more than 450 medals and awards since 1979, and was declared Champion Estate of the Klein Karoo in 1986, 1989 and every year since 1993.

Most wine critics consider the Vintage Reserve Port of Die Krans to be one of the best South African port wines, while its good quality, value-for-money Ruby Port is very popular throughout the country, as well as overseas.

Brothers Boets and Stroebel Nel believe that good wine can only be made from good quality grapes and, therefore, they regard vineyard management as an extremely important part of the whole process. Die Krans won the KWV Vineyard Block Competition in the Klein Karoo in 1995.

The vineyard route on the estate is a 30-minute walk through the vineyards, information along the route explaining several interesting facts to visitors.

A vintners platter is offered during the December holidays. During the rest of the year, lunches can be booked for 10 people or more.

BEVERAGES INCLUDE:
Chardonnay, Chenin Blanc, Late Harvest, Golden Harvest, Cabernet Sauvignon, Pinotage, Tinta Barocca, Ruby Port, Vintage Port, Vintage Reserve Port, White Muscadel, Heritage Collection, and White Jerepigo.

Opening times:
Weekdays: 08:00 – 17:00
Saturdays: 09:00 – 13:00
• Cellar tours can be arranged on request.

Die Krans Estate
P.O. Box 28
Calitzdorp
6660

Tel: (044) 213 3314
Fax: (044) 213 3562

DOORNKRAAL

Doornkraal, where the Le Roux family has been farming for generations, lies at the foot of the Swartberg in the Klein Karoo. This part of South Africa is sometimes referred to by its old name, Kannaland.

When the farm was established a small vineyard was immediately planted between the great stretches of thornbush which characterises this region. For three generations wine was made and brandy distilled, until the present winemaker's grandfather began making sweet wines in 1936.

Gerrit (Swepie) le Roux bottled a dry red in 1978, and in 1986 he and his wife Ann opened a wine house in the veld (grassland) at the side of the road between De Rust and Oudtshoorn, where Doornkraal wines can still be tasted and bought today.

Doornkraal's philosophy is that wine is a gift from God to man and not the other way round. Swepie le Roux is of the opinion that wine must always be a personal choice and that people should have an easy, intimate relationship with wine.

At present 30 ha (74 acres) are planted with, among others, chardonnay, semillon, chenin blanc and muscat frontignan grapes. Among the red cultivars are cabernet, merlot, pinotage and tinta barocca. It is interesting to note that the wines in the cellar are fined with the whites of ostrich eggs, a practice unique to South Africa.

The present winemaker is Piet le Roux, son of the owner of the estate. He produces 19 different wines, of which the sparkling wine, Tickled Pink, is the most popular.

BEVERAGES INCLUDE:
Tickled Pink, Sauvignon Blanc, Chardonnay (from 1998), Merlot, Merlot-Pinotage blend, and Cabernet Sauvignon (from 1998).

Opening times:
Weekdays: 09:00 – 17:00
Saturdays: 08:00 – 13:00

Doornkraal
P.O. Box 104
De Rust
6650

Tel/Fax: (044) 241 2556

MONS RUBER ESTATE

The Mons Ruber Estate is a family concern currently jointly managed by the Meyer brothers. Farming activities are divided between viticulture and ostriches, with wine production dating back to at least 1850, judging from the original wine cellar.

In the early years, however, production centred on brandy. In 1936, for example, there were still eight pot stills in operation.

Witblits (under the tradename Moonshine) and brandy are sold, but the estate produces mainly dessert wine (jerepigo), since climate and soil lend themselves to a sweet cultivar. At the same time it must be pointed out that a good dry red is made of cabernet sauvignon grapes, which also produces a port and a unique jerepigo. Most of the wine from this estate is destined for the wholesale trade.

Mons Ruber has received numerous awards through the years, and produced the Little Karoo Grand Champion in 1977 and 1988.

The farm offers a number of very interesting sites and phenomena such as the striking red hills (*mons ruber* in Latin) which have been declared part of the Natural Heritage Scheme. A hiking trail in the proclaimed area is dedicated to the memory of Raadus Meyer, the winemaker's father.

Visitors can obtain hiking permits and information on local plants and birdlife at the Mons Ruber wine tasting venue.

The historic tasting venue of Mons Ruber houses a display of memorabilia of the royal visit to the farm in 1947, as well as ostrich feather articles created on the estate. The old world charm of the restored 19th-century kitchen should not be missed.

BEVERAGES INCLUDE:
Cabernet Sauvignon Jerepigo, Elegantia, Port, Cabernet Sauvignon Port, White dessert wines like Muscadel Jerepigo, Hanepoot Jerepigo, Regalis and Bonitas, dry red Cabernet Sauvignon and Oonari, and the light dry white Vino.

Opening times:
Weekdays: 08:00 – 17:00
Saturdays: 09:00 – 13:00

Mons Ruber Estate
P.O. Box 1585
Oudtshoorn
6620

Tel/Fax: (0442) 51 6550

SANDKOPPIES (GRUNDHEIM WINES)

Just outside Oudtshoorn lie the vineyards of Sandkoppies, the home of Grundheim wines. Here, five generations of the Grundling family have been farming for more than a century.

The stately pioneer's home harbours mysterious, 160-year-old murals, discovered during recent renovations. These colourful motifs, painted in an unknown medium, are not indigenous to South African folkart and historians are currently researching their origins. The farm also has a historic wine cellar that is over a hundred years old.

Sandkoppies has been producing fine wines for the past fifty years. Today, winemaker Danie Grundling builds on his forefathers' skills and vision. Some of the vines have been growing in the deep, fertile, alluvial soil for eight years. The grapes are allowed to ripen on the vines, hence the distinctive raisin character of the wine. This wine farm is famous for its traditional barrel fermentation process and the absence of artificial colourings and sugar in the wines.

Apart from muscadel and vintage port, Sandkoppies is also renowned for its *witblits* (firewater made in a traditional brandy-still). In addition, Grundheim's family recipes have ensured that, for generations, their home-made liqueurs and preserves have won numerous awards and prizes.

The warm and friendly atmosphere of this remarkable farm is sure to bring you back, time and again.

BEVERAGES INCLUDE:
Sweet dessert wines and port. Witblits, as well as a range of liqueurs and preserves, are also available.

Opening times:
Weekdays: 08:00 – 17:00
Saturdays: 08:00 – 12:00
• Closed on Sundays.

Sandkoppies (Grundheim Wines)
P.O. Box 400
Oudtshoorn
6620

Tel/Fax: (044) 272 6927

The Oranjerivier Wine Cellars (Co-op) Ltd was established in 1965, and its five cellars are all situated along the lower reaches of the Orange River.

The cellars, which came into production over the period 1968 to 1976, are located at the towns of Upington, Keimoes, Kakamas, Grootdrink and Groblersdorp.

Upington Cellar enjoyed its first wine making season, with Jan Neethling as winemaker, in 1968 – after thorough planning by people like Spatz Sperling, winemaker of Delheim, and H. Feil, then of Agrico.

Copious rains during the 1969 season, and a resultant surplus of grapes, compelled the board of directors to consider additional cellars. A cellar was built at Keimoes in 1970 and started production in 1971, with Noel Mouton as winemaker-manager. Grootdrink pressed its first harvest in 1972, directed by winemaker Hennie Sieberhagen.

Abundant rains and the floods in 1974 influenced the decision to build yet more cellars, at Kakamas and Groblershoop, with Matthee van Schalkwyk and Jannie Engelbrecht as winemaker-managers. They came into operation in 1976.

Oranjerivier Wine Cellars (Co-op) Ltd has 750 members producing 90 000 tons of a wide range of grapes annually. The main cultivars are chenin blanc, sultana and colombard. The two red cultivars which fair well in the area are pinotage and ruby cabernet.

Although the vineyards are situated in an arid part of the country, receiving an annual rainfall of only 190 mm (7.5 in), they are all irrigated directly from the river and yield heavy crops.

Due to the high summer temperatures experienced in the area, the sugar content of the grapes is very high too – as a result the area is traditionally known for its fortified wines.

To date the Co-op has received a total of 1 550 awards at wine shows.

BEVERAGES INCLUDE:
Grand Crû, Chenin Blanc, Blanc de Blanc, Colombard, Stein, Late Harvest, Special Late Harvest, Nouveau Blanc, Pinotage and Ruby Cabernet.

Opening times (sales only):
Weekdays: 08:00 – 12:45 / 14:00 – 17:00
Saturdays: 08:00 – 12:00
• Wine tastings can be arranged on request.

Oranjerivier Wine Cellars
P.O. Box 544
Upington
8800

Tel: (054) 331 2186
Fax: (054) 332 4408

JANUARY
St Vincent's Eve Festival (Villiera)

FEBRUARY
Nederburg Pre-Auction Public Tastings
(in major cities)

MARCH
Hanepoot Festival
    Klawer
    Goudini
    Rawsonville
Vineyard Festival (Vredendal)
Weintaufe (Eikendal)
Moonlight Pique-Niques (Boschendal)
Harvest Festival (Robertson/Mc Gregor)
KWV Autumn Concert
Nederburg Wine Auction
Klein Karoo Arts Festival

APRIL
Cellar and Kitchen Festival (Oudtshoorn)
    held during Klein Karoo Arts Festival
Nederburg Auction
Paarl Wine Route Nouveau Festival
Swartlands Train Relay
    (Paarl–Franschhoek)
PPC Spoornet Winelands Train Relay
    (Goudini–Ceres)
Muscadel Festival (Montagu)

MAY
Food and Wine Festival (Malmesbury)

JUNE
Winter Red Wine Review (Cape Town)
Food and Wine Festival (Worcester)
Food and Wine Festival (Swartland)

JULY
KWV Berg River Canoe Marathon
Boschendal Bastille Day (July 14)
Franschhoek Bastille Day
Natal Mercury Wine Week (Durban)
Calitzdorp Port Festival
    (last weekend of the month)
Elsenburg College Wine Auction
    (Groot Constantia Museum)
Vinimark Trade Day (Cape Town)

AUGUST
SA National Young Wine Show (Paarl)
Paarl Young Wine Show
CIWG Pre-Auction and Barrel Tastings
    (always held around Stellenbosch)
Stellenbosch Winemakers' Roadshow

SEPTEMBER
Independent Winemakers' Guild
    Auction (Stellenbosch)
Business Day Festival (Johannesburg)
Waterfront/Argus Wine Festival
    (Cape Town)
Young Wine Show
    Stellenbosch
    Worcester
    Robertson
    Klein Karoo

Young Wine Show (continued)
Orange River
Grootdrink 1
Olifants River
Cape Independent Winemakers' Guild
  Auction (Spier Estate)

OCTOBER
SAA Wine List Awards (venue varies)
Spring Festival (Eikendal)
Spring Festival (Franschhoek)
Blaauwklippen Blending Competition
  (Blaauwklippen function room)
Veritas Awards (Cape Town)
Food and Wine Festival
  (Robertson Valley)
Robertson Valley Countrywide Tour

Food and Wine Festival (Stellenbosch)
Die Burger Wine Festival (Tyger Valley)

NOVEMBER
Cheese and Wine Festival (Bonnievale)
Juliet Cullinan Wine Festival
  (Gallagher Estate)
Worcester Bottled Wine Show
Church Street Festival (Tulbagh)
Stellenbosch Bottled Wine Show
  Port Elizabeth – 19 November
  Durban – 20 November
  Pietermaritzburg – 21 November

DECEMBER
Wine Festival (Mc Gregor)

GLOSSARY

Acid: wine which was spoilt by acetic acid during ageing (tastes of vinegar).

Acidity level: the sharpness or tartness which lends a freshness to white wine.

Ageing: (maturing process) – during which wine, kept in wooden vats, softens and develops its character.

Alcohol strength: usually expressed as a percentage of volume.

Aperitif: drink which stimulates the appetite, like sherry and vermouth.

Aroma: flavour coming from the grape and fruit acid.

Balling: sugar content of grapes is expressed in degrees Balling.

Blanc: white

Blanc de Blanc: white wine made only of white grapes.

Blanc Fumé: dry white wine made of sauvignon blanc grapes, often aged in wood – therefore has a smoky taste.

Blanc de Noir: made from red grapes.

Blending: mixing two or more selected wines or brandies to achieve a desired wine of the right age, character, colour, fullness, alcohol level or sugar content.

Botrytis: (noble rot; noble late harvest) fungus infection; dehydrates grapes, increasing sugar content and flavour.

Bottle age: softening development of a wine after bottling.

Bottle sickness: temporary loss of flavour and bouquet caused by contact with too much oxygen while the wine is being bottled.

Bouquet: the flavour which originates with fermentation and maturation.

Brandy: distillate of wine – strict requirements in South Africa dictate distilling in copper pot stills and a minimum period of wood maturation.

Burgundy: full, dark red, dry wine; originated in Burgundy, France.

Cap Classique: *see* Méthode champenoise.

Cellar: production site for wine; in Europe traditionally built underground.

Champagne: sparkling wine made according to the traditional Méthode Champenoise. By agreement with France, South Africa may not call any sparkling wine made here, champagne.

Charmat: method for making sparkling wine under pressure in a sealed tank.

Claret: red wines from Bordeaux (the name originated in 12th-century England).

Cocktail: appetising drink made from different ingredients mixed in the glass.

Corked taste: unpleasant taste acquired when an inferior cork affects the wine.

Criadera: part of the cellar where sherry undergoes its first maturation.

Crust: deposit on the inside of bottles after the wine has aged for a long time.

Cuvée: French term for blended wine.

Decant: pouring wine out of the original bottle into a carafe, while preventing sediments from clouding the wine.

Demi-sec: half-dry (sparkling wine).

Dessert wine: sweet wine obtained when a small amount of wine spirit or brandy is added to wine to stop fermentation and preserve the grape sugar.

Distilling: process of boiling and condensing the vapours of an alcoholic liquid, resulting in highly purified spirit.

Doux: sweet (sparkling wine).

Dry wine: unfortified (natural) wine; so much grape sugar has been fermented that no trace of sweetness remains.

Fermentation: chemical reaction in which micro-organisms (yeast cells) convert sugar to alcohol.

Fino: palest, lightest, most delicate and generally driest of all sherries.

Flor: yeast cells used to make sherry.

Fortifying: adding brandy or spirits to stop fermentation (result is sweet wine).

Free run: pure juice obtained when destemmed grapes are lightly pressed.

Grape residue: skin, pips and fruit flesh that remain after grapes are pressed.

Jerepigo: dessert wine; high sugar content due to little or no fermentation.

Late harvest: sweet wine made from grapes harvested late in the season.

Lees: sediment formed during fermentation or storage.

Liqueur: alcoholic drink sweetened and flavoured with aromatic extracts.

Magnum: 1.5 l (2.64 pint) wine bottle.

Méthode champenoise: classic method of making champagne by causing a second fermentation in the bottle. Since 1992 the term Cap Classique has been used in South Africa.

GLOSSARY

Mousse: French term for the foam on sparkling wine (indicative of quality).

Muscadel: aromatic grape variety and the sweet dessert wine made from it.

Must: juice of freshly pressed grapes.

Natural wine: (table wine) product of natural fermentation of must to which no alcohol has been added.

Nouveau: refers to young wine made to be drunk early.

Oloroso: semi-sweet Spanish sherry, well aged and amber coloured.

Oxidation: chemical change in wine due to contact with air; usually detrimental.

Perle: between natural and sparkling wine; added carbon dioxide lends a light sparkle.

pH: the neutral point is 7 (water). The lower the reading, the higher the acid. Optimal pH of must and wine is 3,1–3,4.

Port: sweet, fortified wine.

Rosé: blend of red and white wine, or made only of red grapes of which skins are removed before too much colour has been extracted.

Sec: French for dry (sparkling wine).

Solera: (Spanish) ageing and blending sherry in a series of three vats, to obtain consistent quality year after year.

Sparkling wine: effervescent wine.

Special late harvest: dessert wine with a minimum sugar level of 20g/litre.

Stein: semi-sweet white wine.

Sugar: residual sugar which remains in wine after fermentation.

Tannin: essential preservative from grape skins, ensures good ageing.

Tartness: the dry sensation which puckers the mouth, especially in the case of red wines; depends on tannin.

Ullage: space occurring in a vat from wine lost by evaporation or leakage.

Variety: (cultivar) kind of grape used.

Vermouth: grape-based drink, flavoured with aromatic herbs.

Viniculture: vines grown specifically for the making of wine.

Vin ordinaire: everyday drinking wine.

Vintage: when a harvest was pressed.

Viticulture: cultivation of vines.

INDEX

INDEX